KEEP SHOWING UP

Dang, girl! Powerful and practical straight talk in a world that wants you in a twist about marriage. A must-read and re-read. A dose of vitamin T (truth) about what marriage can wonderfully look like when we look more at what God can do in our commuted hearts than what our husband or wife should do for us, more at what God gives to the unit than what we are expecting to get as individuals.

> **ELISABETH HASSELBECK**, wife, mom, television personality, and author of *Point of View: A Fresh Look at Work, Faith, and Freedom*

When you open a Karen Ehman book, you know you're going to find tons of practical suggestions, years of hard-earned wisdom, and a down-to-earth, we're-all-in-this-together approach that is relatable, reliable, and well worth reading. *Keep Showing Up* is all that and more, providing solid biblical direction for getting—and keeping—your marriage on track. Whether you've been married for ten months or ten years, this much-needed resource will help you grow spiritually, even as you strengthen the most important relationship you have on earth.

> **LIZ CURTIS HIGGS**, bestselling author of *Bad Girls of the Bible*

I have been inspired by and grown through every Karen Ehman book that I've had the privilege of reading, but this one quickly became my favorite. Having just celebrated fifteen years of marriage with Mike, I found Karen's words to lovingly convict me and motivate me to re-envision how our differences can actually be the door to a deeper connection with each other and a greater dependency on God. *Keep Showing Up* truly delivers on what the back cover says it will help you and your spouse accomplish together.

> **JEANNIE CUNNION**, author of *Mom Set Free*

Karen Ehman has written the message every wife needs to hear. Whether she's just starting out or has been married for what now feels like a lifetime, there's something for every wife. With humor, grace, practical teaching, vulnerability, and biblical truth, Karen hits on all the hard topics. I see this book restoring marriages that feel dry, empty, shallow, or just tired. I see it as a longstanding resource for counselors or pastors to pass on to women who just need a wise friend to encourage them to keep showing up.

NICKI KOZIARZ, wife to Kris and bestselling author and speaker with Proverbs 31 Ministries

Marriage is more than just a promise; it's a commitment. It's vowing to each other that you are life partners and will walk through life hand in hand, side by side, regardless of the ups and downs you will surely face. *Keep Showing Up* will help cultivate your marriage during the good, the bad, and those moments you threaten to sleep on the couch! ;)

LAUREN McBRIDE, lifestyle blogger at www.laurenmcbrideblog.com

I've seen firsthand in my research how one person's simple actions can make or break a marriage. This book provides an excellent, actionable map for how we women can help our marriages to fly even when it gets rough—or boring. We can't change our man, but when we work on us, everything changes! Karen Ehman has written another practical, charming winner.

SHAUNTI FELDHAHN, bestselling author of *For Women Only*

Karen Ehman has such a down-to-earth and real-life style of writing. *Keep Showing Up* is relevant for everyone from the engaged woman to the one who has been married for thirty years and beyond. She offers practical advice backed with scriptural truth to encourage you to help your marriage and yourself. Her use of personal stories and humor will draw you in, but the substance of her words will have you ready to go to work on building a better relationship. I can't recommend this book enough.

KELLY STAMPS, popular blogger at kellyskornerblog.com

Keep Showing Up will make you wonder if Karen Ehman has been secretly living in your home, watching and listening to your marriage. We found that so many of her stories resonated with our own. Insightful, fun, and incredibly practical!

PATRICK AND RUTH SCHWENK, founders of FortheFamily.
org and TheBetterMom.com and authors of *For Better or
For Kids: A Vow to Love Your Spouse with Kids in the House*

The apostle Paul says the profound mystery of marriage can be summed up in the relationship between Jesus and his jacked-up bride, the church. The inexplicable fact that Jesus keeps showing up and doesn't go anywhere when we continue to ignore and flat-out dismiss him is one of the most stunning pictures of the gospel of grace. In this wonderfully transparent, practical, and Jesus-centered book, my friend Karen Ehman makes much of Christ by exalting marriage to its proper place as a portrait of grace painted with the brushstrokes of our failures and halfhearted attempts at doing the right things.

NOEL JESSE HEIKKINEN, pastor at Riverview Church
and author of *Wretched Saints: Transformed by the
Relentless Grace of God*—and Karen and Todd's pastor

Keep Showing Up isn't a long list of unreasonable to-dos for wives to undertake. Instead, Karen Ehman comes alongside to coach and encourage you toward a gospel-centered marriage. From newlywed to seasoned wife, every bride should read this book.

KELLY R. SMITH, MrsDisciple.com

Whether newly married, never married, or married so long you can't remember not being married, *Keep Showing Up* is a must-read! With grace, humor, and her own personal experiences, Karen Ehman demonstrates how even a strong union of two can crumble by the wrong mindset of one. This book challenges us to examine our hearts and offers a fresh perspective to help leave crazy behind and stay crazy in love.

REBECCA LYNN DIKEMAN, writer and blogger
from Arizona, married for fifteen years

Keep Showing Up is a blessing of a book. I've been married for almost eleven years, and Karen Ehman's book has taught me so much. Yes, it may step on your toes! But it reminds us that marriage is not for selfish ambition but calls us to be selfless—to put our spouse's needs above our own and to love in the "agape" way. In doing so, it helps us be molded into who God created us to be and to love like him!

ASHLEY RHODES, married for nearly eleven years

Wow! This book truly exposes the raw, honest truth about the many ups and downs in marriage. It provides a convicting—and redeeming—solution that will allow you to become a God-honoring wife: *examine your own heart*. *Keep Showing Up* challenges you to stop looking at your spouse and at other external factors that make marriage hard, and instead start evaluating your own heart as you allow God to enable you to love like Jesus.

BAILEY SEXTON, married for three years

Preparing for my recent wedding, I didn't want to hear more "congrats on finding happily ever after." Instead, I wanted real advice from someone living in a real marriage. In this book, Karen Ehman gives rarely found raw truth in a way that is refreshing. Her willingness to honestly paint the realities of marriage strengthens my "new wife" heart in a way Cinderella never could.

JACKIE SLOT, married for five months

As an almost-newlywed, I found *Keep Showing Up* to be a godsend. Reading each page was like finding treasure troves of pure gold nestled among catchy phrases, humorous anecdotes, and candid and sincere advice—all filtered through the lens of the Bible. I feel so much more prepared as I delve into this new adventure called marriage. However, this book provides valuable information to men and women in all stages of life and with all relationships, not just the one between spouses. I'm making it my mission to *keep showing up*, today and every day, with everyone who crosses my path.

MACEY NESTER, became Mrs. Mitchell Ehman in 2018

KEEP SHOWING UP

How to Stay Crazy in Love
When Your Love Drives You Crazy

KAREN EHMAN

ZONDERVAN®

ZONDERVAN

Keep Showing Up
Copyright © 2019 by Karen Ehman

Requests for information should be addressed to:
Zondervan, *3900 Sparks Dr. SE, Grand Rapids, Michigan 49546*

ISBN 978-0-310-34768-2 (audio)

Library of Congress Cataloging-in-Publication Data

Names: Ehman, Karen, 1964- author.
Title: Keep showing up : how to stay crazy in love when your love drives you crazy / Karen
    Ehman.
Description: Grand Rapids, MI : Zondervan, [2019] | Includes bibliographical references. |
Identifiers: LCCN 2018052331 (print) | LCCN 2019000412 (ebook) | ISBN 9780310347651
    (ebook) | ISBN 9780310347644 (softcover)
Subjects: LCSH: Wives--Religious life. | Marriage--Religious aspects--Christianity.
Classification: LCC BV4528.15 (ebook) | LCC BV4528.15 .E39 2019 (print) | DDC
    248.8/435--dc23
LC record available at https://lccn.loc.gov/2018052331

Cover illustration: Shutterstock
Interior design: Kait Lamphere

Printed in the United States of America

19 20 21 22 23 24 25 26 /LSC/ 15 14 13 12 11 10 9 8 7 6 5 4 3

To Marcia Stump,
a wife who faithfully models for me
how to keep showing up and keep showing Jesus

CONTENTS

Important Note: This book was written with the average marriage in mind that has its share of heartache, misunderstandings, and normal marital spats. If you are dealing with a more serious issue, such as porn addiction or adultery, or if the conflict you experience over any issue causes arguments that escalate quickly or even frighten you due to verbal abuse or physical harm, get help! Reach out to your pastor if you have one. Or you can find a Christian counselor in your area by visiting ccn.thedirectorywidget.com. Or if you are in physical danger and being abused, please stop what you are doing now and call the National Domestic Abuse Hotline at 1-800-799-7233 or visit www.thehotline.org.

Also, I realize that not all of you reading this are on your first marriage. For a variety of reasons—whether beyond your control or due directly to your own choice—you are no longer with your first spouse and are part of a remarriage situation. Please know that, in advocating for you to continue to show up in your relationship and do the hard work of behaving in a biblical manner in your marriage, I'm referring to your current marriage. Do not misinterpret my encouragement to hang in there in your relationship as a condemnation for not staying married to your former spouse. No wagging fingers from me—just grace and a reminder that God's mercies are new every single day.

ONE

WHERE DOES A WIFE GO TO RESIGN?

*There can be no deep disappointment
where there is not deep love.*
DR. MARTIN LUTHER KING JR.

*Whom have I in heaven but you? And earth
has nothing I desire besides you. My flesh and
my heart may fail, but God is the strength
of my heart and my portion forever.*
PSALM 73:25–26

Why is this so hard? I can't do this anymore! I cried out to God as I sat cross-legged on the bedroom floor of our very first apartment, my eyes stinging with hot, salty tears. Out in the living room on a hand-me-down couch sat my husband, bewildered himself, unable to handle his wife's unstable emotions. I'm sure he was also thinking that this marriage wasn't at all what he'd imagined it would be.

I was a brand-new bride of just six weeks, fresh off the honeymoon and with our moving boxes barely unpacked. Our thank-you notes for the wedding gifts hadn't even been sent!

But already I had buyer's remorse. Or I guess more accurately, "bridal remorse." All I knew was that this "happily ever after" thing was not so happy after all. I already wanted to resign from my newly acquired position of "wife."

My husband and I met during our sophomore year of college. On our Midwestern Christian campus, students came to get a dual degree—one in their chosen field of study and one in the department of matrimony, snagging not only the title Bachelor of Arts behind their name but also Bachelor/Bachelorette-No-More. I'd received my BA in social science as well as my "Mrs." degree within three weeks of each other. I was pleased with the first one, having worked hard to graduate with honors. My diploma hung proudly on the wall in our postage-stamp-sized apartment. The second degree I now wished I could give back.

I never envisioned being unhappy in my marriage. Not for a moment. Of course, during our dating days, Todd and I had experienced some disagreements and spats. However, these lovers' quarrels always concluded with us smooching and making up, more in love than ever before. (Cue the sappy music and puppy-dog eyes.) But much to my dismay, the first few years of my marriage were rocky and rough.

I had imagined a relationship of big-screen marital bliss. Candlelit dinners. Surprise bouquets of wildflowers. Holding hands at the movies. Moonlit strolls along a lovely path. Then the tidal wave of reality hit.

Instead of the candlelit dinner, it was burnt roast. When he *once again* came home late from work, I wrongly interpreted it as him caring little about my culinary efforts. We didn't get to the hand-holding at the theatre much because we couldn't make up our minds about which show to see. And there were strolls along the path all right—all alone down the dimly lit streets in our neighborhood, just after I stormed away from my beloved following yet another dispute.

Facing the fresh, harsh reality that marriage wasn't all roses and rosy was a slap in the face emotionally. It left me wondering if I had made a horrible mistake when it came to the choice of my mate.

Yes. Maybe that was it. I had chosen the wrong person. This line of thinking certainly entered my mind. But my brain didn't just play a spirited round of the blame game, asserting that my husband was the problem. I also entertained the thought that there was something wrong with *me*; that although I had read every popular Christian marriage book out there at the time—curled up on my college bunk bed, highlighting until my fat pink pen ran out of ink—I just wasn't cut out to be a wife. Both these options left me feeling disheartened and miserable.

I wiped my eyes and then tried to give myself a little pep talk, assuring my fretting brain that everything was going to be all right. Maybe I was just overreacting. After all, there wasn't a major issue in our marriage. There hadn't been any infidelity. We weren't in deep financial trouble. Neither of us had a major crisis in our career. There wasn't any verbal or physical abuse. A few couples we'd gone to college with were experiencing one or more of those serious issues. I thought perhaps reminding myself of this fact would make me feel better about my current unpleasant situation.

But it didn't. No matter how stellar and convincing a self-lecture I could muster up, I couldn't see past the pain and sorrow of my current condition. This was not the newlywed life I'd wanted. Marriage was supposed to be magical. Fulfilling. Fairy-tale-like. Not the stress-inducing, bawl-my-eyes-out, fresh disappointment I was currently drowning in. Weren't we supposed to be crazy in love? What in the world went wrong?

WHY MARRIAGE IS SO STINKIN' DIFFICULT

Now that I've had a couple decades of marriage under my belt, I recognize that my newlywed disillusionment was not unique to me. There are lovers all over the globe who dive excitedly into marriage only to realize, after taking the matrimonial plunge, that their relationship as husband and wife is not the heavenly home front they'd imagined. So just what is the problem? Why is obtaining a marriage of harmony and bliss so much harder than falling in love and dating? Is it the sex? Meddlesome in-laws? Financial pressures? Conflict over the kids? Is it just the sheer daily grind of navigating work and home responsibilities while dealing with differing perspectives and personalities? Yes, it's all that and more. And while I can't possibly hope to touch on all those marital trouble spots in one short book, I can focus on one crucial half of the marital equation: *you.*

You heard me. I said you. Not your husband. Not what he is or is not doing—but you.

But first, let's look at some of the underlying issues that make marriage today so difficult.

We Have Sky-High Expectations for Marriage

From the time I was a little girl, I had an idealistic view of marriage. My neighbor Ann and I would sometimes spend the afternoon on my front porch playing with our Barbie dolls. Between the two of us we had several female dolls but only one Ken doll. So we had to take turns sharing the only hubby we had.

When it was my turn for Ken to be my Barbie's hunk-of-a-husband, sometimes the duo spent a quiet evening at home in the Barbie DreamHouse. Other times they ventured off in the fancy aqua camper on an exciting summer vacation. Or perhaps they splashed around in the makeshift swimming pool Ann and I had created from a shallow Tupperware bowl. But one thing they never did? They never fought.

The husbands and wives on television rarely fought either. Or if they did, the conflict was resolved within a span of thirty minutes. Many of the people I knew in real life—neighbors, relatives, teachers—seemed to have their marital acts together. No, not all of them. I also knew of couples who either had gotten divorced or were in the process of doing so. But at that time, this was rare. And I surmised *my* marriage would not be like those.

Setting the bar too high in marriage—surmising that yours will be free of conflict, full of romance, not a struggle but a breeze, sets you up for disappointment. Let's ditch any idealistic notions and opt for some realism instead. There will be troubles from time to time—maybe even a lot of the time. But while we can't change our circumstances, we can change our perspective. We can expect such times and grow despite them.

Our Culture Doesn't Support Marriage or Encourage Couples to Stay Married

In fifth grade I remember being able to count on one hand the number of classmates I knew whose parents were *not* together. And society as a whole, for the most part, seemed to support and encourage marriage. There were some who bought into the old "a woman needs a man like a fish needs a bicycle" philosophy, but they were women I only read about or saw on the news. They weren't the actual women in my life who were influencing me. The women *I* knew believed in marriage.

I have often wondered about the institution of marriage in the past. Was it easier to be married years ago when staying together was expected and divorce was taboo? Today, do we have the same outside support that marriages had in the past?

And, if not, has losing that outside support made staying married even more difficult?

I love historical buildings. Give me a good tabletop book, full of glossy photographs of architecture from the past, and I will snuggle up under a blanket and dreamily peruse it for hours. One of those ancient, intricate architectural styles is the cathedral. I was challenged once to think about how a cathedral's structure illustrates the connection in years gone by between marriage and society.

Most cathedrals have a unique component to their architecture called a flying buttress. Buttresses were designed to hold the walls and roofs of cathedrals together by exerting pressure from the *outside*. Over the years, however, builders learned to tuck away the reinforcements *inside* the structures or even hide them within the masonry walls. They no longer had to rely on exterior construction components to hold the walls together. They counted on what was inside the building to make them stand strong and tall.

Now consider marriage in our current culture. There just aren't many outside forces acting upon it in a positive way any longer. In fact, sometimes the opposite is true. Marital breakups are winked at. Shrugged off. Even celebrated sometimes. Serial marriages aren't rare anymore—especially in Hollywood.

Because of our culture's shift from supporting marriage, expecting unions to last, it's easier to just give up when things become strained. I've been told by a marriage counselor that roughly 50 percent of the people who walk down the aisle think in the back of their minds that if they become disenchanted or even bored, they can just throw in the bouquet and walk away. Then they can set off looking for a new partner who will make them have all the tingly feelings again. Or if they consider dissolving the marriage, they may not be met with a slew of people urging them to hang in there and do the hard work of strengthening their relationship with their spouse. Instead, they may be thrown a divorce party instead.

Yes. You read that right. This is actually a thing! A quick peek at Pinterest will even give you all sorts of ideas for hosting one, such as how to make a "Divorced Diva" sash for the new "Ex-Mrs." to wear, how to create clever invitations for her friends that read, "I do. I did. I'm done," or instructions for playing the game "Trash the Dress" with the soon-to-be-single gal's wedding gown.

How disgraceful.

Because we don't always feel support from the outside, it can contribute to what we ourselves think about our marriage. Will we knuckle down and press on, recognizing that marriage is rough but oh-so worth it, or will we too decide to just fold up shop and move on instead? Why not? It seems plenty of other people are doing it, and being celebrated as they do.

And I'm not talking about always actually getting a legal divorce. Sometimes we just become emotionally detached—divorced in our affections, distant, and disillusioned. *Emotional divorce* is accepted, often even expected, in our culture. It's the stuff sitcoms are made of.

Everybody seems to agree: marriage is just too difficult. And the quickest, easiest solution? Too often, it's divorce.

We Are Fallible Creatures in a Fallen World

Now, please don't misinterpret my words and conclude that I believe there are never good reasons for divorce. Or that remarriage is wrong. A quick scroll through my phone contact list of close friends would prove just the opposite! I have walked with many dear friends through painful, sometimes unwanted, divorces. And I have happily danced at the weddings of friends when they remarried after surviving a divorce. Although I am a strong proponent of marriage, I realize we live in a fallen world. Not only are there biblical grounds for divorce, there are also serious cases of abuse. Certainly, women often endure horrific—even dangerous—conditions in their marriages that traumatize them and jeopardize their children, and they need to seek help to escape.

Marriage is difficult simply because we are fallible creatures who sometimes make seriously poor choices. Although most of my friends who have experienced divorce were the victims—having spouses who had affairs and then left them—there are a few who decided to divorce for reasons not outlined in Scripture. They didn't hang in there when times got tough. They broke up their marriage due to their own affair, or even for a trivial reason. Some just decided they were not happy anymore. And since they thought marriage was designed to make them happy, they threw in the towel, left their spouses—and in some cases, their children—and set out to start a new life. Years later, they realized what they did was wrong, but there was no way to go back because they or their first spouse had remarried. For these people, there *is* forgiveness and a fresh start. It has been exciting for me to see them gain a renewed perspective on marriage, one that lines itself up with Scripture.

We deal daily with the results of fractured relationships and sinful choices. But the good news is that there is a God who redeems and makes all things new. So please know that when I speak of hanging in there during the difficult times of marriage, I am not subtly implying anything about any marriages from your past. No whispers of shame ruffling through these pages. No implications of guilt. Just God's wonderful mercies that are new for each of us every single morning.

What else contributes to the reality that forging a harmonious marriage isn't a walk in the park? How about our clashing personalities and demeanors? This has been especially true in my own marriage.

OPPOSITES ATTRACT, OR OPPOSITES ATTACK?

The day my husband and I walked down the aisle over a quarter century ago, a thought gripped my mind, threatening to knock the joy right out of our ceremony, replacing it with fear and worry instead. You see, just weeks earlier, as we sat in my pastor's office for one of our premarital counseling sessions, we'd been told that the results of our personality-and-strengths profile tests revealed a sobering assertion—less than 5 percent of the marriages consisting of two people with our specific profiles end up lasting.

Lovely.

My husband and I were college sweethearts who loved the Lord—and each other—immensely. We couldn't wait to become a family, forge ahead in ministry in our local church, and, we hoped, welcome children into our home someday. However, the pastor's pronouncement dangled ever in my mind, a dark cloud of potential doom that I feared would turn into a storm of sadness. As a child and young adult, I had a front-row seat watching the marriages of several couples I dearly loved end up in divorce court. I didn't want my husband and me to be the next ones standing in front of the judge.

However, as I observed those marriages and others that ended as well, they showcased for me an important truth I have seen played out repeatedly over the past three decades: it takes two people to create a strong Christian marriage. Unfortunately, it takes only one person to break it up.

I determined not to go forth in debilitating fear of what might happen once we'd recited our vows. I could do nothing to control the behavior of my husband should he decide to leave me someday. However, I could determine that—with God's help—I myself would be a person who kept my marriage vows, even when my husband's habits or personality differences drove me nuts, and despite seasons when the storms of life would rock our relationship. My actions toward my spouse could reflect the unconditional, steadfast love of God to those who were watching us, both up close and from afar. I knew it would not be easy, but I was determined to try.

As our marriage marched on, no serious sins or major storms of life presented themselves. It was more just an overall feeling of frustration with the way my husband and I are so different. In how we process problems. How we think things should be done around the house. How we interact with people. And don't even get me started with the thermostat!

I loved that my fiancé was laid-back and agreeable. However, about three months after he became my husband, I began to interpret his easygoing, often indecisive demeanor as passivity. I hated when he was passive. It caused me to get aggressive. I guess you could say we had a passive-aggressive marriage!

Meanwhile, my fiancé loved how during our dating years it seemed I could talk to anyone about anything. But about three *days* into our honeymoon he wondered when I was ever going to shut up! (He says if I go before him, he will put a period on my tombstone because he will then know I am finally finished talking!)

These aren't our only differences. We spend our money and our time differently. We clean the house differently. We don't always agree on parenting decisions. We communicate differently. When conflict arises, he would prefer to wait until . . . *well, never* to address it. In contrast, I would have chosen to discuss it yesterday had I known it would happen today! Why, we can't even decide on a Pandora station to listen to on a long drive! (He chooses smooth jazz, while I opt for the Johnny Cash station.)

It is true that—especially in our dating years—opposites

attract. A soft-spoken, reserved person might be attracted to a significant other who is decisive and talkative. An introvert might go for an extrovert. A fast-paced, city girl may dream of romance with an unhurried country boy. Unfortunately, as relationships move forward, opposites also tend to *attack*. As a result, the habits and characteristics that we found endearing about our significant other during courtship often are the exact things that drive us nuts later!

This phenomenon arises because—for all of us—as our strengths get carried to extremes, they morph into weaknesses. The superb communicator becomes an annoyance who rambles on and on, monopolizing conversations and boring their listeners (that's me). The methodical planner becomes overcontrolling (also me). That happy-go-lucky, life-of-the-party person becomes a haphazard spouse who forgets details and appointments. The laid-back, agreeable person might hesitate from making decisions, coming across as passive.

With every strength there is a flip side. And if the flip side is not dealt with, it can even lead to the disintegration of the marriage relationship. Journalist Mignon McLaughlin attested to this when she once claimed, "If you made a list of reasons why any couple got married, and another list of the reasons for their divorce, you'd have a ... lot of overlapping."[1]

WANTING OUR OWN WAY

These personality disparities between husband and wife become the soil where conflict takes root. We can't for the life of us understand why our spouse handles financial decisions differently than we would. Or why they stack clean dishes the ... *ahem* ... wrong way. (The right way, of course, being how *we* would do it.) Or we blink in disbelief at their unconventional method for painting a room, which seems totally backward to us. These dissimilarities greatly intensify during the parenting years. So many arguments pop up when mom and dad have entirely different opinions about how to discipline their darling dependents.

However, what really makes a harmonious relationship so elusive is that, due to our sin nature, we are wired to think only of ourselves. Or at least to think of ourselves first. I'm not suggesting that we are all complete nuptial narcissists, but we do tend to look out for good ole number one.

The biblical writer James wisely asks, "What causes fights and quarrels among you? Don't they come from your desires that battle within you?" (4:1).

We want our own way. We want our spouse to let us *get* our own way. And striving to get it leads to conflict. Conflict, when not handled properly, causes friction and frustration. When we are part of a marriage experiencing such struggles, we begin to wonder what is wrong. *Why can't we just get along and be happy?*

Ultimately, each marriage—and the challenges it brings—is unique. However, two realizations I've come to discover over the past three decades of marriage to my college sweetheart have greatly helped me to keep showing up and keep working on our relationship. These truths are not profound, but they are profoundly true: *marriage is hard* and *it's not about me.*

Haven't we been programmed to believe just the opposite? Especially in this age of social media, where creatively orchestrated engagements materialize right there before our eyes on our phone's tiny screen. Or Pinterest-perfect husbands and wives appear on our laptops in the form of smiling spouses, eating delicious food in picturesque surroundings, with the look of love dancing in their eyes. We get the impression that if only you find Mr. or Mrs. Right, a harmonious marriage will ensue.

Marriage isn't hard. Marriage is a breeze! Well, as long as you picked the right person.

And, *of course*, we think marriage is all about us. It is what will finally make us happy—just as Barbie was with Ken cruising down life's merry lane in the cherry-red Barbie convertible! When we find that perfect soul mate, we'll achieve relational heaven on earth. We'll look deep into the eyes of our significant

Marriage is hard and it's not about me.

other and romantically utter, à la Jerry Maguire, "You complete me." (I'm so sorry. My nineties are showing.)

How glorious it would be if all these things were true. But the tough reality is that marriage *is* hard and it's *not* at all about us. And it's really not even about our spouses. Well, then, just who *or what* is it about then?

WHY GOD PLAYED TINDER WITH ADAM AND EVE

Have you ever wondered why God invented marriage? I mean, aside from the obvious reason that a husband and wife could produce babies who would grow up and get married and produce more babies, so the world would keep spinning and spawning new life. I mean, after all, God is God. He could have come up with any number of scenarios for producing new human beings while allowing time to go marching on. Why did he decide to initiate the institution of marriage? And why-oh-why didn't he also cause it to be a tranquil and effortless affair? Let's crack open the Bible to see if we can figure it out.

The first mention of the covenant of marriage is in Genesis, the Bible's first book. After spending six days creating the heavens and the earth, vegetation and animals, and finally Adam, the very first man, God rested from his work. Then God looked at

Adam and determined that he was not only alone but also lonely. We pick up the story in Genesis 2:18: "The LORD God said, 'It is not good for the man to be alone. I will make a helper suitable for him.'"

Whoa, now. Hold the phone. Or at least let it roll over to voice mail. Helper? A *helper*? Really? What a weak and wimpy word! It makes me think of Hamburger Helper—that dish you quickly throw together when supper is near but you haven't been anywhere near your kitchen that day to make it. "Oh, here. This box of helper will do. It won't be very good, but it will suffice in a pinch." But is this word used in Genesis—translated "helper"—a weak "it'll do for now" word?

I've heard and read many explanations of this word's meaning over the years. Some people have asserted that the woman was made to be a subordinate, almost less-than in importance, assistant to the first man, ready to carry out his wishes in complete submission and without question. Others have made light of the situation, suggesting that Adam was so incompetent he certainly needed a helper. Why, he probably couldn't find his way around the Garden of Eden and would never dare to stop and ask for directions. And so, ta-da! God created Eve. Not to be a subordinate but because Adam would surely never survive without her.

Let's look for a moment at the intended meaning of the word we read today as *helper*.

In Hebrew, the language in which Genesis was first written, the word *helper* is the word *ezer*, a masculine noun that does, at its core, mean "to help." However, many biblical scholars assert that *ezer* originally had two root words with two varied meanings; each was based on an initial guttural sound, but over time blended into one word. One sound meant "strength," and the other meant "power." If so, the meaning of *ezer* has nothing to do with a weak, subordinate counterpart. In fact, if you grew up in a church that was in the habit of singing hymns on Sunday morning, perhaps you recognize this root word from the second stanza of "Come, Thou Fount of Every Blessing" by Robert Robinson, where it reads, "Here I raise my Ebenezer; hither by thy help I'm come."

What's an "Ebenezer"? (I mean aside from the first name of Charles Dickens's famous character Scrooge!) The Ebenezer was a stone raised into the air by the Old Testament prophet Samuel (1 Samuel 7:12) intended to remind the Israelites of God's help for them in their struggles. We also see the word *ezer* in Psalm 33:20, used to describe God himself helping us in our time of trouble and turmoil. In fact, the word is used twenty-one times in the Bible, most often in a military sense and referring to God's prevailing help. God, the epitome of strength and aid; God who will fight for us in battle. So, no thoughts of a weakling woman whose only job is to prop up Adam and be in his shadow, okay? Eve was a powerful partner for Adam, a strong and invaluable ally who fought the battles of life standing right beside him.

How God created Eve also teaches us something about the marital relationship. We resume the story in Genesis 2:21–23:

> So the LORD God caused the man to fall into a deep sleep; and while he was sleeping, he took one of the man's ribs and then closed up the place with flesh. Then the LORD God made a woman from the rib he had taken out of the man, and he brought her to the man.
>
> The man said,
>
> "This is now bone of my bones
> 　　and flesh of my flesh;
> she shall be called 'woman,'
> 　　for she was taken out of man."

I love that Eve was fashioned from matter taken from Adam's side. She wasn't crafted from a bone taken from his foot, signifying that she was to be a slave bowing down at her husband's feet. She wasn't brought into being by using part of his head, implying perhaps that her brains are better than his and he'd better let her make all the decisions. She was taken from his side. A partner. An equal. And today, husbands and wives stand side-by-side as each other's ally as they travel through life together.

Of course, there are many other Scriptures that give a glimpse into God's plan for marriage. Consider the very next verses—Genesis 2:24–25: "That is why a man leaves his father and mother and is united to his wife, and they become one flesh. Adam and his wife were both naked, and they felt no shame."

A man leaves his family of origin. He is joined to his wife. This uniting is both spiritual and physical. The two humans become one flesh. And, they are naked and yet feel no shame.

Normally, our being stark naked in front of another human being makes us hesitant and reluctant—or at least it should! Not many of us would like to go parading around for all to see wearing nothing more than our birthday suits. (I still hate going to the doctor for my annual physical even though I've had the same wonderful doctor for more than twenty-five years!) But with our spouse, we can be naked and feel *no* shame or embarrassment. Not only that, we can be both *naked* and *nekkid*. *Naked* means you have no clothing on. *Nekkid* means you have no clothing on—and you're up to something. (At least that's what I've been told.)

So, the husband and wife are united in flesh. But being united spiritually? What's up with that? We find our answer when the words of Genesis 2:24–25 are echoed in the New Testament book of Ephesians: "'For this reason a man will leave his father and mother and be united to his wife, and the two will become one flesh.' This is a profound mystery—but I am talking about Christ and the church" (Ephesians 5:31–32).

The husband-wife relationship is supposed to illustrate the relationship between Jesus and the church, pointing others to its importance. Elsewhere in Scripture, the body of believers here on earth is referred to as the "bride of Christ." The sacred truth shown in this metaphor of marriage is that God destined there to be an enduring union between Jesus and all those who place their trust in him. Our earthly marriage as Christians paints a vibrant portrait to the watching world of this divine design. God's blueprint is for Christ and the church to be one (1 Corinthians 12:13; Galatians 3:28). Our relationship with our spouse is meant to mimic this pattern of unity.

So why would God ordain that our relationship as husband and wife point people to the connection between Jesus and the church? I mean, couldn't they just read about it in a Bible or flip on a TV preacher who would give them the gospel message—the account of God sending Jesus to earth to die a sacrificial death, pay the penalty for our sins, and offer us a place in heaven for eternity with him?

Yes, some people *do* receive the gospel by those methods, but the timeworn saying is true: "More is caught than is taught." God, in his divine wisdom, also desires that people on earth will catch spouses living out his redemptive plan. My pastor, author Noel Heikkinen, summed it up perfectly in a recent sermon when he declared, "Biblical marriage preaches the gospel to

> *Your marriage is a message, and people are watching you preach.*

our culture by modeling Jesus in a lifelong covenant between one man and one woman, characterized by sexual exclusivity, complementary servant roles, and the ongoing sacrifice of self."

So, it isn't just pastors who deliver a sermon. Your marriage is a message, and people are watching you preach.

CLOSE ENOUGH FOR COMFORT

When I became a Christian in high school, I was able to spend valuable time with two women who took on the task of mentoring me. Occasionally I spent afternoons in their homes after school. Sometimes I stayed overnight. I was able to watch up close their behavior as wives. I saw them interact with their spouses in situations of tension and conflict. I observed them having fun. I witnessed them expressing fear for the future as they dealt with a medical condition or a financial strain in the family. And all the while, I was taking copious mental notes.

I saw them live out scriptural concepts such as putting others before yourself, practicing patience, granting grace, offering forgiveness, and pursuing true reconciliation. They made their husbands, kids, and homes a priority while not neglecting their own desire and need for outside interests. I didn't see them retaliate when treated wrongly. Instead, they directly but gently pointed out any offenses. They sought to behave in a way that honored God in their relationships. They weren't perfect, but the way they always endeavored to represent Christ had a deep effect on me.

Their eagerness to extend their arms and welcome me into their ordinary family life changed my life. This front-row access to Christ-honoring marriages made me desire to have such a relationship too. These women didn't preach. They just lived. And I caught the lessons they taught through that living.

Learning about how a wife should act and react wasn't the only benefit. I was also introduced to the relationship of Christ and the church. I was intensely drawn to the gospel when I saw its redemptive story lived out in their homes, a living example of God's plan for humankind. I got to experience firsthand how much he loves the church—so much that he laid down his life for her.

Now, one interesting fact about the two homes where I saw this lived out before my eyes by wives who loved their husbands and the Lord: *those marriages did not last*. (Hang with me here. I have a point.) I hope that learning this doesn't cause you to disregard the important lessons I learned by studying these wives. The unhappy reality that these marriages didn't last introduced me to the truth I mentioned already: it takes two people to make a great marriage. Unfortunately, it takes only one to break it up.

Both these wives meant their marriage vows. They were not faultless, but their perspective was in keeping with Scripture. While fully determined to do their part in creating a sacred marriage that would last, their spouses stopped working toward this aim. In each case, the husbands had affairs and ended up divorcing their wives.

While this was a sad turn of events, it also highlighted for me an imperative life lesson—one that I want to stress to you strongly.

Everything in life—even your life as a wife—all comes down to you and Jesus.

You cannot make your spouse behave a certain way. You can't control his behavior or micromanage every situation. The only thing you can control is yourself—your response to others, your attitude, your behavior. In fact, that is one of the prayers I have for you as you read further—that you will focus on your own behavior rather than run to your husband to beat him over the head with this book and get him to change his erring ways.

It all comes down to you and Jesus.

This is not a manual about how to manipulate your man so he instantly morphs into Mr. Magnificent. It isn't a step-by-step formula that will ensure that, if you take certain actions, your husband will follow suit, and then everything will be a basket full of bliss in your home.

This book is really about you and your relationship with God.

- Will you dare to love, serve, and sacrifice, doing it only for an audience of One?
- Will you continue doing the hard, relational work of marriage *regardless* of how your husband responds?
- Will you apologize earnestly when you behave poorly and forgive fully when you are the one wronged?
- Will you be willing to wipe the slate clean, keep showing up, and keep showing Christ—not only to your spouse but to all the watching eyes in your little corner of the world?

Remember, it all comes down to you and Jesus. He sees your heart. He knows your motives. He feels your sorrow and shares in your suffering. You will not be held responsible for the conduct of your spouse, only for your own behavior.

When we understand the reality of the challenges of marriage and hitch it to the truth of God's purpose for marriage, we can discover the encouragement— and the strategies—that will prevent us from hanging up on our marriages and will empower us with ways to hang in there instead. Rather than fighting *in* our marriage, we discover how to fight *for* our marriage. Instead of resigning as "wife," we can re-sign our commitment to be "all in."

> **Will you dare to love, serve, and sacrifice, doing it only for an audience of One?**

Yes, the first few years of marriage were tough. And even now, three decades later, I don't have a husband who is everything I could ever want in a man. And he certainly doesn't have a wife who is the woman of his dreams. But do you know what I have discovered that makes me extraordinarily thankful and hopeful?

I have discovered that having—and being—an imperfect spouse keeps me on my knees.

You see, if I were a perfect wife and had a perfect husband who could meet my every need, I wouldn't sense my need for Jesus. And if Todd were a perfect husband who had a flawless wife who never yelled or nagged (not that I ever do those things!), he would have no need for a Savior. So that's why I am grateful I have a husband who drives me nuts (and he, a wife who drives him even nuttier!). Because . . .

It drives us both straight to Jesus.

And it allows these two college-kids-turned-middle-aged parents to beat the stacked-against-us odds. So, tonight on our thirty-second anniversary, we celebrate big with grilled cheese sandwiches and glasses of iced tea on our back deck. Our marriage is ordinary, yet it's part of an important mission: to keep showing up, forgiving, and reflecting the gospel to those in our sphere of influence.

> **Marriage is when a man and woman become one; the trouble starts when they try to decide which one.**
>
> *Anonymous*

Your marriage can do the same, my friend.

Don't resign. Re-sign.

Just keep showing up.

TWO

Embracing Your Sandpaper Spouse

*Before you marry a person, you should
first make them use a computer with slow
internet to see who they really are.*
WILL FERRELL

*Be completely humble and gentle; be patient,
bearing with one another in love.*
EPHESIANS 4:2

When I first married, I never realized that marriage involved so much math. I don't mean actual arithmetic—long division, negative integers, or the calculation of square roots. I mean these little equations that form in my mind, creep into my thinking, and lead me to form strong opinions about my husband's behavior. The format they follow is this:

Husband's behavior = His thoughts about me.

I'll bet you have your own unique calculations regarding your husband's actions. Here are some I latched onto early in our marriage:

A husband who doesn't talk when we're driving somewhere together in the car = A husband who is uninterested in what's going on in my life.

A husband who doesn't introduce me to his coworker when we run into him at the supermarket = A husband who is embarrassed by my appearance and apparel (unwashed hair up in a ponytail and unwashed yoga pants).

A husband who picks up fat-free half & half at the store = A husband who wishes I were more fat-free.

Now, these little equations could all be easily explained if I would just allow my guy two minutes to do so. If I would listen long enough to understand his actions—rather than instantly hurtling to conclusions—I would discover that I had come to some very wrong deductions.

It isn't true that Todd is uninterested in what's going on in my life when we're rambling down the road together—my mouth also rambling. He's just being quiet because he is thinking about something that happened at work. Or maybe he's pondering how many blocks before his next turn, since the last time we drove to this destination he missed it—most likely because I was yakking! Also, the truth is that he isn't a big talker. He'd rather drive in silence—unlike me, who thinks every little gap of silence on a twelve-hour road trip simply must be filled!

As for the encounter with his coworker, Todd was not embarrassed by my appearance. He just didn't know that coworker very well and couldn't remember his name. Since introducing us would reveal this fact, he became nervous and decided not to make the introduction at all.

And Todd wasn't making a veiled comment about my weight

by bringing me fat-free half & half. He just doesn't know his way around the dairy case at our local grocery store as well as I do. He simply spied a carton sporting the words "half & half," grabbed it, and headed to the checkout lane.

All these little miscommunications and wrong deductions left me totally offended when they shouldn't have. They caused me to lash out, instigating a little (okay, ginormous) spat that did not make for a happy home front.

Years later, I have gotten better—though not stellar—at letting the poor man explain himself so these untrue views of what I surmise he's thinking don't happen. However, these irksome equations are elementary when compared to the equation that has caused the most turmoil in our marriage. It's the calculation that trumps all others, one I bought into as soon as we walked down the aisle and into life together, one I've struggled with for the better part of three decades. Are you ready for this doozy? The equation is:

Different = Wrong

Do you also subscribe to the notion that different equals wrong? This notion rears its ugly head in marriage *all the time.* This word *different* applies to so many facets of marriage.

Our personality is usually unlike that of our husband. Our upbringing may be dissimilar. Our choice of television programs doesn't always match. We may pick different restaurants to dine at, and let's not even talk about which way to hang the toilet paper on the roll!

Most of all, our thought patterns are not similar. The way we filter information or process a problem may be completely contrary to our husband's approach. In fact, I'll bet this calculation of "different = wrong" is especially troublesome when it comes to how your husband thinks—and then acts—differently than you do. It is so prevalent. And so daily. You see it come into play . . .

around the house
in dealing with the in-laws (YIKES!)
in parenting the kids
in matters of communication
in areas of romance and intimacy
in how you spend money
and on and on it goes

I spent many years arguing with my husband, either in a slightly joking but get-the-point-across tone or with my voice nearly raising the rafters—trying to convince him that his different way of doing things wasn't just different; it was flat-out *wrong*. It wasn't until my good friend Mary cared enough to address this issue with me one day that I realized my equation was all wrong.

Different isn't wrong. It's just . . . *different.*

Mary and I have been friends for a couple decades now. We've been each other's accountability partner in a few areas of life— for instance, we keep each other on track with daily Bible study and prayer; we discuss how to parent our children with love and forgiveness rather than with guilt and control. In short, we've granted each other the right to honestly—but gently—point out blind spots that may be hindering our relational or spiritual growth. The area of life in which we've most helped each other, and held each other accountable, is marriage.

One day, when I was once again complaining about my husband's "wrong" way of doing something, Mary made a statement I've never forgotten. In her sweet and encouraging voice she said, "Oh, Karen, if you and Todd think exactly the same about everything and handle every situation in the exact same manner, then *one of you is unnecessary.* The only person who would do exactly what you would do in any given situation—is you. Your marriage doesn't need two Karens; it needs one Karen and one Todd."

Her words to me that day were the beginning of a monumental shift in my marital thinking. Different isn't wrong. It's just different.

This swing in philosophy didn't happen overnight. Nor without great effort on my part. If there were hidden cameras set up in my home, they'd still catch me pacing back and forth, preaching out loud to myself, *Different is just different. It is not wrong. Different is just different. It is not wrrrr . . .* (suddenly spies the hubby doing something his own way) *What are you thinking?! You're doing that all wrong!* (See, I told you it doesn't come easy for me!) I imagine it will be the same for you, if you've also supposed that different is wrong.

A new line of thinking can emerge when we realize that my friend Mary is spot-on. Your marriage wasn't designed by God for each of you to be a carbon copy of the other when it comes to how you attack life. Your differences should be not just noticed but embraced. Decide that you will see the opposite (and even contrary) ways you and your spouse think and act as beneficial to your marriage. Different can be delightful. And the differences between a man and a woman in marriage are to be celebrated, not spurned.

In his book *What Did You Expect? Redeeming the Realities of Marriage*, Paul David Tripp describes the delight of differences:

> One way God establishes beauty is by putting things that are different next to each other. Isn't this exactly what God does in marriage? He puts very different people next to each other. This is how he establishes the beauty of a marriage. The moon would not be so striking if it hung

in a white sky; in the same way, the striking beauty of a marriage is when two very different people learn to celebrate and benefit from their differences and to be protected from their weaknesses by being sheltered by the other's strength.[1]

The first woman elected to the United States House of Representatives back in 1916 was Jeannette Rankin, who happens to be a relative in my husband's family tree two generations ago. She also recognized the importance and beauty of the different genders when she asserted, "Men and women are like right and left hands; it doesn't make sense not to use both."[2]

Yes, dear cousin twice removed, Jeannette. You were entirely right.

'TWILL BE ALL RIGHT (IF YOU'LL BE LIKE TWILL!)

In high school I took a home economics course. I fared rather well with the cooking and cleaning. What tripped me up was sewing. Attempting to sew a straight seam—and doing a dreadful job—prevented me from receiving an A. The article of clothing that wrecked my grade? A navy-blue vest made from twill.

Twill is a woven textile with a pattern of diagonal and parallel ribs that combine to create a finished product having two distinct sides. The fabric technically has a front and a back side, unlike plain weave, whose two sides are exactly the same.

Due to this unique weaving process, twill is very hearty and durable. It shows fewer spots and stains than other materials because it is highly resistant to soils. Its differing sides also allow the threads more flexibility; therefore, twill fabrics are softer and more pliable, and they drape better. The uneven surface of twill—as compared to the smooth surfaces of plain weaves—results in a raw material ideal for sturdy work clothing and military uniforms. Denim is a twill. So is chino, first used for military uniforms in the mid-nineteenth century.

Our marriage relationship can be like twill. When two very different spouses come together as one, yet each retains their distinctiveness, the results can be a thing of strength and beauty. Like twill, your marriage can shed the spots and stains of irritations and transgressions, and it can be flexible and pliable, shaping itself to suit both of your needs. Your marriage will then be not only as durable as denim, but it will also be strong enough to fight the Enemy. (Psst . . . the enemy is Satan—not each other!) Our two-sided and oh-so-different relationships can be crafted to endure.

ON GRIT AND GRACE

Another creative process that can help us understand our marital differences is one I didn't learn about in home ec. This one I discovered in Mr. Cassidy's industrial arts class!

In the eighth grade, I was in need of another elective. Because my school district wasn't huge, my choices were limited. I could've sung in the choir, painted and thrown pottery in art class, or hung out in Mr. Cassidy's room learning the ins and outs of working with wood and leather. I opted for industrial arts.

Now, the reason I chose it had nothing to do with the fact that the class was 95 percent boys. (Okay, I lie.) At any rate, I leaped in and learned. My first project was a stamped leather keychain that displayed two painted pink flowers and the word *Mom*. The flowers have faded over the decades, but my mom still uses the keychain. My second project was a tad more complicated: a paper towel holder made out of pine.

For this assignment, I had to learn to measure and cut with

a band saw. (I can still hear Mr. C's voice warning, "Measure twice. Cut once.") I am a safety freak and can concoct worst-case scenarios in about three seconds flat, so I was glad when that dangerous part of the job was finished and I still had all ten fingers attached.

The last steps of the assignment were to nail and glue the pieces together and then stain the pine wood a dark walnut shade. However, before that could happen, the most tedious—and time-consuming—task had to take place.

Sanding.

Now, I'd like to report to you that this was easily done on an electric belt sander. But again—small-school problems. We had to do it by hand. With rather small squares of sandpaper. *Totally* by hand. My eighth-grade self didn't relish this stage of the project. I was concerned it could mess up my freshly painted purple fingernails!

I started with a coarse grain of sandpaper to remove the major wood splinters sticking out of the ends of the dowel where I'd cut it with the band saw.

Once finished, I went back up to the materials center to grab a new piece of sandpaper. This time, it was a medium grade. I used it to give a sweeping once-over, grind down any imperfections in the wood, and assure that the pieces would fit together well when I glued them.

Finally, I grabbed some squares of the finest grade sandpaper, designed for ultimate smoothing, and polished the wood to a sleek surface. However, because these pieces clogged up very quickly, I constantly had to toss out a square and grab another to keep going. Imagine my frustration! But . . .

At the end of two weeks, I had a completed—and surprisingly functional—paper towel holder, fashioned solely by little ole me.

Over the years, I've come to think of Todd as my sandpaper spouse. He just plain rubs me the wrong way sometimes with his oh-so-different-from-me ways of doing things.

Having a spouse who faces life differently can often tempt us to attack each other. But what if we were to flip the script and view things that rub us the wrong way as tools that can help rub off our rough edges? Tackling first our biggest flaws, which are most evident. Then the smaller issues that arise over time and also need smoothing out.

Proverbs 27:17 states, "As iron sharpens iron, so one person sharpens another." If your kitchen knife is dull, you sharpen it by grinding it against a rough stone, not by rubbing it on cushy cotton. In the same way, the rough patches in our personalities can help us to sharpen each other in the areas of love, compassion, and patience—mostly patience!

My husband's slower-paced decision making causes me to pause and pray *before* I forge ahead, and it helps me consider other options I might not have thought of initially. My verbal processing encourages my husband to talk through issues rather than stuff his feelings inside where they can fester and later explode. And our different philosophies teach us deference, perseverance, and a new perspective.

My friend, actress and author Candace Cameron Bure, and I were chatting about marriage the other day. She and her husband, Val, a Russian-born former pro hockey player, recently celebrated their twenty-second wedding anniversary—a milestone in itself. But couple that with the fact that she is in show business, where people change partners faster than a speed-dating session, and this is an accomplishment even more remarkable!

I asked Candace why her marriage has not only lasted but thrived in a culture where so many couples barely make it a decade, deciding their spouse no longer makes them happy or citing the ever-popular, "I don't love them anymore" reason for calling it quits.

"Marriage is not about our ultimate happiness," she replied. "That is a lie from the devil. Marriage was made to refine us, to grow our character. It exposes the worst in us so that we see the need for humility, grace, forgiveness, and, most of all, our need for Jesus in our marriage. We've been fed the American dream—that marriage is all about self-seeking happiness. I often wonder, *Why would* anyone *stick it out if they weren't bound to a biblical understanding of marriage?* If you think marriage is for pleasure and happiness, you will always be let down. Marriage was made to refine you and make you more like Jesus."

We can decide to embrace the grit-and-grace, back-and-forth smoothing process of our marriage. Or we can resist the polishing process. Trust me. Clutch it close! Let it refine you, making you more like Jesus as it does. As we are rubbed the wrong way, we can respond in grace. Forgive. Move ahead.

Ask God what he's trying to teach through the bumpy patches and places in your relationship. And realize that you are not alone.

While we're on the subject, you know, don't you, that it isn't just certain aspects of your husband's behavior that bother *you*? The reverse is also painfully true, whether you and I care to admit it or not.

EVERYBODY'S GOT SOMETHING

My intense irritation at my husband's actions didn't visibly show. Since his mother was in the back seat of our car, I was careful to remain calm. However, I did sneak a darting glance toward him—a dagger that accurately conveyed how very much I hated what he'd just done.

His dire offense? Wait for it . . .

He failed to use his blinker when changing lanes.

I am a by-the-book driver. My kids chuckle when I dutifully use my blinker before turning into our driveway, even when no one is around—which is nearly 99 percent of the time, since we live near the end of a cul-de-sac. Therefore, it aggravates me when my dear husband sometimes behaves as if turn-signal usage is completely optional.

This particular day, we were shuttling my mother-in-law to her doctor appointment. As I sat in the waiting room, my mind began to tally, one by one, other perfectly irksome things I didn't like about my man's behavior.

He leaves the closet and cupboard doors open. Open!
He didn't return the stapler to its proper place when he
*   finished using it the other day.*
He never remembers the details of our conversations.

As each scenario popped into my mind, I grew more and more annoyed.

Meanwhile, on a TV in the waiting room, a meteorologist was predicting an ice storm later that afternoon and warning drivers to stay home. An elderly woman sitting next to me pooh-poohed the warnings. "Everybody's got somethin'," she declared.

I asked her just what she meant by that. "Well," she elaborated, "when we lived in Kansas, it was dust storms and tornadoes. Then, during the few years we lived in southern Florida, we had to prepare for hurricanes. And when we were stationed in California, oh what a drought we had that one year. Like I say," she said again, "everybody's got somethin'."

My waiting room friend's observation snapped me to attention. *Why, oh, why do I let certain aspects of my husband's personality and conduct bother me so easily? Surely I do things that drive him equally crazy! Undoubtedly, I sometimes irk or offend him with my behavior.* Indeed, "Everybody's got somethin'"—some behavior, quirk, practice, or habit that wreaks havoc on others, tempting them to become slightly irritated or even all-out furious.

Proverbs 19:11 states that "good sense makes one slow to anger," and it is a person's "glory to overlook an offense" (ESV). In the original Hebrew, the word *glory* conveys "beauty, honor, splendor" and even "adornment." It unearths for us this line of thinking: our patience in passing over an offense—refusing to speedily go from zero to furious over the actions of others—adorns us with true beauty and honors them.

I'm not saying it's easy. However, it is the right—and righteous—thing to do. Why? Because we mirror the gospel when we perfect the art of overlooking—excusing another's irksome behavior and loving them anyway.

So how about it? Does your beloved sometimes get on your nerves or under your skin—or maybe even both? Does your response to his behavior leave no doubt about your level of frustration? How about trying a new approach—intentionally overlooking that irritating behavior?

Yes, that means we keep our cool. We don't say a word, but we *smile instead* and *love despite*. In the great love chapter of the Bible, 1 Corinthians 13—which is read at countless weddings—we find these words:

> Love is patient, love is kind. It does not envy, it does not boast, it is not proud. It does not dishonor others, it is not self-seeking, it is not easily angered, it keeps no record of wrongs. Love does not delight in evil but rejoices with the truth. It always protects, always trusts, always hopes, always perseveres.

Now, there's enough material in that power-packed chunk of Scripture to write a dozen books on marriage. I want us to focus on just three phrases:

1. "Love is patient."
2. "It is not easily angered."
3. "It keeps no record of wrongs."

Oh, man. There have been—and sometimes still are—so many times where, if those three phrases were used as a measuring stick to see how I'm treating my husband, I would flunk.

I have very little patience with him. And I can understand why the King James Version of the Bible doesn't say, "Love is patient." It says it "suffereth long." Hello? Who likes to suffereth? And if I *do* have to suffereth, I want it to be overeth in a jiffy, not to taketh a fortnight or two.

Next up: I'm often easily angered. (Come on? Getting all bent out of shape and wailing like a maniac over a blinker not being properly deployed?) And, sad to say, I have been known to keep a record of wrongs. A very detailed and properly filed-away record, thank you very much. I not only can tell you something Todd did that offended me; I can tell you where we were standing and what he had on when it happened!

Yes, I have a terrible habit of getting historical. Yes. I don't mean hysterical. I mean historical—dragging up incidents and wrongs from the past and then flinging them in my husband's direction during a heated discussion or talk about them in a sarcastic way when I'm trying to make a point. (Please, someone tell me I'm not alone!)

Aren't you thankful that God doesn't treat us this way—getting so angry and losing patience with us, or dredging up our past sins and offenses? In fact, he does just the opposite:

But you, Lord, are a compassionate and gracious God,
    slow to anger, abounding in love and faithfulness.

Psalm 86:15

The Lord is not slow in keeping his promise, as some understand slowness. Instead he is patient with you, not wanting anyone to perish, but everyone to come to repentance.

2 Peter 3:9

Or do you show contempt for the riches of his kindness, forbearance and patience, not realizing that God's kindness is intended to lead you to repentance?

Romans 2:4

For as high as the heavens are above the earth,
    so great is his love for those who fear him;
as far as the east is from the west,
    so far has he removed our transgressions from us.
As a father has compassion on his children,
    so the LORD has compassion on those who fear him.

Psalm 103:11–13

Even when we blow it, God lovingly chooses to forgive our sins when we repent. The least we can do is to intentionally overlook the peculiarities and annoying habits of our mate, remembering that we have a nifty collection of them ourselves. In fact, this concept is found in another verse that can serve as a great lens through which we view forgiveness in marriage: "Be kind and compassionate to one another, forgiving each other, just as in Christ God forgave you" (Ephesians 4:32).

Why do we show kindness when irritated, compassion when

wronged? Why do we choose to forgive, wiping the slate clean and starting fresh in our relationship?

Because this is EXACTLY how God treats us.

SEVEN SHORT SERMONS TO PREACH TO YOURSELF

So, what does this look like realistically? Are there any concepts we can cement in our minds to help us to love like Jesus as we embrace the grit and grace of living with our sandpaper spouse?

Yes, there are. First . . .

1. Choose your love. Then love your choice. When our kids were younger, they were always thrilled when we took them out for dinner at a restaurant. At a restaurant, they didn't have to eat whatever Mom had cooked or Dad had grilled. Instead, they could order anything they desired. When they did, however, we made them finish what they'd chosen. No looking at your brother's chicken strips and then deciding you didn't want spaghetti after all. Choose what you love, but then love what you choose. That was our message at the restaurant.

We would do well to adopt this concept in our marriage.

Once upon a time, you chose your partner. Now, years later, you need to keep choosing him daily by displaying love despite how you feel. By allowing the good characteristics of our spouse to outweigh the behaviors that aggravate us or even the recurring issues that exasperate us, we choose love, reflect the gospel, and, over time, build a strong, caring relationship.

2. Lose the attitude. Keep the marriage. Pastor Chuck Swindoll has a great perspective on the part that attitude plays in our life: "I am convinced that life is 10 percent what happens to me and 90 percent how I react to it, and so it is with you."[3] Losing your negative attitude and adopting one that understands that life doesn't always go your way—which includes the life lived with your spouse and the frustrations it sometimes brings—make all the difference.

So . . . chin up. Smile on. Forge ahead. Don't clothe yourself with a drab, complaining attitude that drags you down. Wrap yourself up in a cheerful, encouraging attitude that lifts you—and others—up.

3. To make marriage work, you have to work at your marriage. Love is not merely an attitude. It takes action as well. Fashioning a healthy and loving relationship is not for the faint of heart. It takes tenacious work to make a marriage work. However, the reward is in the work as well. President Theodore Roosevelt aptly observed, "Nothing in the world is worth having or worth doing unless it means effort, pain, difficulty . . . I have never in my life envied a human being who led an easy life; I have envied a great many people who led difficult lives and led them well."[4]

I love that! Especially when I think of the marriages I've observed over the years that seemed to be especially loving, vibrant, and successful. When I've gotten to know one or both spouses in such marriages, I've discovered that their relationships didn't just fall neatly into place. Those couples put in a lot of hard work, consistently wrestling through difficulties and changes over the years. Forgiving often. Fighting fair. Realizing that to make marriage work, you have to work at your marriage.

4. Make your differences work for you, not against you. When I was a young girl, I loved plush toys. One of my favorite stuffed animals was called Pushmi-Pullyu (pronounced "push-me pull-you")—a character from the *Dr. Dolittle* movie based on the book by Hugh Lofting. In the book version, it was a cross between a unicorn and a gazelle; in the movie version, it was depicted as a two-headed llama joined by one body. But rather than this anatomical setup causing trouble—with each end going its own way, trying to drag the other along for the ride—the two heads of Pushmi-Pullyu worked in tandem.

This unusual beast typically used only one of its heads when talking. It used the other for eating its food. This novel arrangement allowed it to eat and speak at the same time, thereby avoiding a scolding for talking with its mouth full! It could walk, talk, and eat just fine, functioning without difficulty due to its two-heads-work-together ways.

Although we as spouses may have our heads in contradictory places, we too can learn to cooperate and collaborate. While marriage takes work, it is less work when we are rowing the nuptial boat in the same direction rather than working against each other in a battle of wills, going nowhere. When we stop viewing each other as the enemy and realize we are on the same team, we can channel our efforts into communicating with a three-pronged goal of understanding, coming to a compromise, and then working together to succeed.

5. Specialize to maximize. Perspective changes everything. When you stop viewing different as wrong, you can perceive how having varying viewpoints, skills, and even non-strengths (my husband and I have learned to refer to each other's weaknesses as "non-strengths"; doesn't that sound so much better?) can be advantageous to your marriage. You just need to learn to specialize and maximize.

Todd and I have learned to divvy up responsibilities based on strengths. He is a detail guy who is observant and thorough. He pays the bills—on time and online—and makes the appointments for the repairman or the cable gal to come to our house when needed. He also researches and purchases home and auto insurance for our family. (Oh please! I'd rather have a root canal!)

My strengths lie elsewhere. I'm a big-picture idea slinger who loves interacting with people. I also have a great memory.

(Which my hubby hates when I use it to get historical!) So, I do the communicating with teachers and coaches, as well as with extended family members when it comes time for a get-together. I'm also the one who remembers to send the cards and make the calls for birthdays, graduations, and anniversaries.

We split up household tasks and dive in to get them done, remembering that it isn't a competition and recognizing that there will be give and take, especially when one of us has more on his or her plate than usual. I may be under a book deadline or have a parenting responsibility that leaves me feeling stretched thin for time. Todd may be putting in overtime at the factory. When this happens, the person with more white space on his or her schedule picks up the slack, knowing the other will do the same another time.

6. Get on your knees—quickly and often! Oh, sisters—this is a whopping one! Trying to deal in a godly manner with a spouse whose conduct drives you crazy will require lots of prayer. Lots. Of. Prayer. You'll need to pray for that long-suffering patience to overlook an offense. To ask for wisdom in knowing the best way—and the best time—to approach a subject. You may even need to fling yourself on your bed, begging God for help, *before* a massive blowup materializes.

Our prayer shouldn't be, "Oh, Lord—please change him!" Our prayer should be focused on our *own* behavior as we ask the Father to help us control our own actions; to graciously respond, not overreact; to display godly characteristics when we interact with our husband; to let God do the work of refining us, through our sandpaper spouse; and to give thanks for the progress we will see both spiritually and relationally as we turn to God in prayer.

And finally . . .

7. Show love to your man for no other reason than just because he is your husband. It is true with spouses—and also with children—that we make a powerful statement when we grant grace and show love for no other reason than that they are ours. This notion hit me in church one day as my pastor read about the baptism of Jesus by his cousin John: "As soon as Jesus was baptized, he went up out of the water. At that moment heaven was opened, and he saw the Spirit of God descending like a dove and alighting on him. And a voice from heaven said, 'This is my Son, whom I love; with him I am well pleased'" (Matthew 3:16–17).

I'd read this passage dozens of times, but that day it hit me. God verbalized his love for his Son *before* Jesus had performed any miracles or healed any sickness. No water-turned-wine phenomenon had occurred yet. No feeding of the multitudes from just a couple of loaves of borrowed bread. God didn't lavish love on Jesus because of his performance. He loved him and was pleased with him *just because he was his Son.*

CHANGE IS POSSIBLE

Recently I was munching on some jalapeño popcorn, catching up on the news, when NASA reported some startling findings. After spending almost a year in space, one of their astronauts, Scott Kelly, had an unusual change in his body. His DNA had actually been altered.

Kelly has a twin brother named Mark. The two men exhibited matching DNA before the trip to space, but now their DNA no longer matched. When the genetic matter of the two was compared, it was discovered that 7 percent of Scott's genes had changed. When tested two years following his return to our planet, those genes *still* had not returned to their normal state. NASA stated that the excursion's 340-day stay was considerably longer than a typical six-month deployment to space. While it was known that a person's genes may slightly change while they are in space, what was surprising is that his genes *stayed* altered. Somehow spending a long time in the heavens changed Scott at his very core.[5]

When dealing with our oh-so-different spouses, we may think we can never develop new habits or make progress in our verbal exchanges with them. Perhaps in the past we've allowed their behavior to get on our very last nerve, and then we lashed out. Or maybe we aren't the sort who gets visibly angry; instead we let our displeasure well up inside and come across in a classic case of the silent treatment, giving them a cold shoulder so icy it can freeze boiling water.

> *Keep your eyes wide open before marriage, half shut afterwards.*
> *Benjamin Franklin*

When we've developed a repeated pattern of interacting with our beloved over the years, it can become part of our relational DNA. It is ingrained. Entrenched. Our frustration grows as we bemoan the fact that we can never change. And it's true. We can't. Not on our own.

We can only change the same way that Scott Kelly did—by spending time with our mind in the heavenly places. We do this when we allow the Holy Spirit to infuse our soul with Scripture—studying God's Word and aligning our behavior with what it teaches us.

God's Word can help us . . .

- give the benefit of the doubt
- listen before lashing out
- temper our tempers
- understand that different is not wrong
- discover that different is, in fact, delightful
- ultimately act in love

In other words, accurately reflect the gospel to a watching world. And more importantly—to a watching husband.

Will you join me in thanking God for sandpaper spouses? Rather than our differences driving us crazy, may they drive us all straight to our knees.

It's time we let spending time with Jesus alter our relational DNA.

10 WAYS
TO LOVE YOUR SANDPAPER SPOUSE

Let's face it, sometimes our spouse just plain gets on our nerves or rubs us the wrong way. Whether it's personality differences or the way we tackle tasks around the home, it can be a setup for frustration, anger, and conflict in our relationships.

Here are ten ways to be intentional in showing love to your spouse—even on the days when he is driving you totally nuts! Take time to try one out today.

1. Time travel. Let your mind wander back to when you first met—and fell in love with—your husband. What qualities did you most love about him? Take a few minutes to reminisce and then let your husband know what it is about him that first attracted you. Either tell him in person during a quiet time with no distractions, or hand-write him a letter pointing out the character qualities you loved most about him—and still do!

2. Find the flip side. It is a fact that any strength, carried to an extreme, can become a weakness. However, the flip side is also true. Often a weakness can be tethered back to a strength. So try to look for the flip side of your spouse's annoying quality. Instead of complaining that he is indecisive, point out his patience when a decision needs to be made. Rather than grumble about his over-controlling ways concerning how the garage is organized, compliment him about how neat it is. If you look for the flip side of something that bothers you, you just may discover something good.

3. Do his job. Give your husband a break this week. Does he normally take out the trash? You do it instead. Is he the one usually responsible for vacuuming out the vehicle and taking it through the car wash? Surprise him and do it instead.

4. Send him off. Send your husband off—either by himself or with a few of his friends—to do something he enjoys doing that you do not. Get him tickets to a sporting event, concert, or auto show. Make up a coupon to send him off on an entire day of fishing. Buy him a gift card to a sports-themed restaurant so he can take a buddy there to order barbecue wings and watch the big game.

5. Bring up his childhood. Find a time to talk with your husband, asking him about his childhood. What was his favorite toy or board game? How about the sports team he most loved rooting for? Then head to an online auction site such as eBay to try to purchase an item from his childhood. What fun it will be when he opens it, bringing back a flood of fond memories.

6. Leave a treat. Here's an easy one: leave his favorite snack or candy either on his pillow where he will discover it before bedtime or on the dash of his vehicle where he will see it in the morning before he goes to work. Make sure to leave a little note with it telling him something that you love about him.

7. Rally the troops. Gather the children (or poll some of your spouse's closest friends) and come up with a "Top Ten List" of things people love about your spouse. Read it aloud to him, late-show style, beginning with number ten and counting down. Be sure to have it typed nicely on a piece of paper for him to have as a keepsake of what others love about him.

8. Make a memorable meal. Is there a particular meal your spouse loves? Homemade chicken pot pie his grandma made, his aunt's famous lemon meringue pie, or a scrumptious seafood strudel from a fancy restaurant you went to on your honeymoon (my husband's fav!)? Track down the original recipe (or a similar one from the internet) and whip up a delicious meal.

9. Send something special delivery. Arrange to have an Edible Arrangement, a batch of cupcakes, or a box of sausage sticks and cheese delivered to his office on an ordinary day—just because. Sign it, "From Your Not-So-Secret Admirer."

10. Pray and say. Set an alarm on your phone to pray for your spouse at a specific time every day. Once you've prayed for him, shoot him a quick text telling him so and sharing what your requests to God are on his behalf. If you aren't praying for your spouse, who is?

THREE

A TRIO OF TROUBLE

*Many marriages would be better if the
husband and wife clearly understood
that they are on the same side.*

ZIG ZIGLAR

Live in harmony with one another.

ROMANS 12:16

I sometimes hear people joke about the history of arguments in their marriage, revealing that their very first fight was on what was supposed to be their dreamy, romantic honeymoon.

Oh, really? You don't say?

I can top that. Our first spat was at the altar, and it was all inconveniently caught on tape.

The closing of our wedding ceremony incorporated a popular element of the weekly church services in my denomination at the time: the congregation, before departing ways at the end of worship, would sing a chorus set to the tune of "Edelweiss" from *The Sound of Music*. It went like this:

May the Lord, mighty God, bless and keep you forever.
Grant you peace, perfect peace, courage in every endeavor.

Lift your eyes and see His face, know His grace forever.

May the Lord, mighty God, bless and keep you forever.

A sweet enough song, right? (Well, except that my denomination soon found out it was illegal to put your own words to the tune of a Broadway show. Gulp!) Nonetheless, the chorus did not prove to be a sweet ending to our marriage ceremony. It was smack-dab during this musical score that our first spat as Mr. and Mrs. busted out.

I envisioned the end of our ceremony this way: Todd and I would be holding hands and facing our congregation—having just shared our first smack on the lips as husband and wife.

The congregation would be standing and smiling, some of them shedding tears of happiness at seeing this darling young couple. I would look out and see my parents. My favorite aunt. My childhood friends. They would all be smiling right back at me. What I wasn't prepared for was what I would spy out of the corner of my right eye.

There, standing next to me, was my new husband. However, the look on his face was not one of elation. He looked as if he were at a funeral, not our wedding.

I immediately was embarrassed. I wanted him to whisk that sour look off his face and replace it with the proper look of ecstasy over marrying his new, beautiful, blushing bride. (At least I hoped people thought I was blushing rather than know the truth that the red look on my face was from my blood beginning to boil!)

I gently squeezed Todd's hand and whispered under my breath, "Smile." He ignored me. The second squeeze was more intense as I repeated my command that he alter his countenance to reflect a suitable expression of starry-eyed bliss. The second time I told him to smile, he answered back under his breath,

"I *am* smiling," and then a weak grin began to slowly wash over his face.

Later, when we discussed it, he told me he *had* been smiling, but his face started to hurt from holding it in the same position for so long. And thus, for a few brief seconds, he ditched the smile to rest his facial muscles. It just so happened I looked over at that exact time and wrongly deduced he had been frowning through the entire send-off song.

This slight fight was just the first that would take place during our inaugural year, as we tried to find our footing as husband and wife. There would be others. The ones I remember most vividly found me weepy one afternoon on a paddle boat in the middle of Corey Lake because of something Todd had just said, pouting through a home-cooked supper in our first apartment, and fuming in the front seat of our silver Volkswagen Rabbit as we navigated home from his parents' house more than an hour away. But the point of this book isn't to win the contest of "Most Domestic Disputes in the First Twelve Months of Matrimony." (Just go ahead and plead no contest. I'm the hands-down favorite.) No, the point of my telling you of all these squabbles is far more important.

The conflicts centered around one or more of three repeating components. Oh, I didn't figure this out all on my own. I stumbled across it one afternoon while helping my husband in his job as the youth pastor of our first church.

For one of the youth meetings, we had a local Christian counselor come to chat with the teens about developing healthy relationships with their parents. I so wish I could remember the energetic speaker's name so I could give her proper credit. I don't. (She had on super-cute gold sandals. Does that count?) However, I do vividly remember the three main points of her talk, even though twenty-five-plus years have passed since I profusely took notes that day in the spiral-bound blue notebook I still had from college. (How I wish I still had it to see what other truth bombs I recorded from her and her years of experience.)

What she taught the teenagers that day also applies to pursuing a healthy relationship in marriage.

Often, we hear the experts assert what they believe are the most common causes of conflict in marriage. It might be finances. Perhaps parenting issues or arguments about who does what around the house. Competition with technology—a rather new but large problem. Of course, sex regularly is thrown into the mix. But what I heard from the counselor that day gave me a very different perspective.

The things I just mentioned might be recurring topics of conflict. But what this counselor taught us is that there are three common threads that threaten to tangle our attempts to converse with another person, *no matter the topic*.

They are baggage, expectations, and perceptions.

If I were a betting woman, I'd wager that you will have the same "Aha!" moment I had that day as we explore this trio of trouble that often wreaks havoc with our relationships. Let's untangle them one at a time.

WHAT'S IN YOUR CARRY-ON?

As part of my ministry, I often fly. Not every week, but at least once or twice a month. While at first it may seem glamorous to be jet-setting about the country, in actuality, traveling can be a drag. Especially when it comes to packing.

When packing, you have to be particular. And you have to know the rules so that you don't accidentally wear or bring along something "forbidden." So, I make sure my liquids are all under three ounces each, neatly nestled together in a quart-sized plastic bag. I have my electronics placed strategically where they are easily accessible when I go through security. I've learned over the years not to wear certain items of clothing, especially those that have metal rivets or excessive decorations of the glittery sort. These seem to set off the alarm at security, making me the winner of a private pat-down.

While I try to be conscientious when packing, taking only what's necessary to ensure a successful trip, sometimes, inadvertently, items migrate their way into my luggage that I did not intend to take with me. Usually, this was when my children were small, and my suitcase was open on our bedroom floor for a few days as I gathered needed items. A stray plastic block, ponytail ribbon, or stuffed turtle might end up coming along for the ride.

When we enter into the covenant of marriage and begin to forge our relationship as husband and wife, each of us brings along some emotional baggage. Baggage we tote into our marriage consists of unpleasant experiences from our past we can't seem to get over, unhelpful thought patterns we've developed over the years due to past relationships—especially familial ones—and even the views of ourselves we've formed as a result. The symbolic image is that of a person lugging all the disillusionments, wrongs, and even sometimes abuses of the past around in a weighty load. These patterns of behavior, often unconsciously carried around, will influence our marriage if we aren't aware of them—and ready to address them.

Some of this baggage we packed ourselves over time as our thoughts formed about people, places, processes, and situations. Other pieces were tucked away in our totes by others when we allowed them to make us feel a certain way about ourselves, our choices, or our relationship skills—or our lack thereof.

As a result, we each enter into our marriage with several suitcases stuffed so tight that the zippers might burst open, catapulting the contents everywhere. And each carry-on, each tote bag, each oversized roller that exists emotionally holds a unique set of items. Each person's personal baggage is unlike anyone else's and certainly is different from what our spouses have lugged along.

Then comes the day when we hit a bump in the road while riding beside our spouse in the marriage carriage. What happens to our baggage then? It is then that we reach in and grab an item—not because it is needed to make the bumpy situation better, but because it feels familiar. And because we assume our thinking about it is true. We draw it in, hold it close, and allow it to dictate our feelings.

Just as a quick online search shows numerous colors, sizes, and shapes of actual luggage, emotional baggage also comes in many forms. It may be the notion that you feel you are fat because, as a once chunky child, the neighborhood kids teased you while your siblings stood by and said nothing. Or maybe you're hesitant to contribute ideas to conversations because years ago, when you took a course in college on ideation and brainstorming, the professor pointed out in front of the class that you lacked originality and your verbal contributions to the daily discussions were not of value. Did a partner in a past relationship make fun of your slightly crooked teeth or a coworker make an offhand comment about your lackluster memory? These experiences could leave you with a certain impression you just can't shake off: I'm fat, unoriginal, ugly, or stupid.

Baggage shades our view of ourselves and of others and can magnify a simple fight, turning it into World War III. This happens often unbeknownst to our beloved. They don't realize we are hauling out old feelings and wrongly assuming that our current spouse also thinks the same thing of us.

Baggage is bad. But as bad as it is, it isn't the only issue that can exacerbate our interactions with our spouse. There is a second culprit in this trio of trouble. And this one doesn't just have its roots in the past. It is often perpetual. This relational nuisance is known as "expectations."

NOT-SO-GREAT EXPECTATIONS

My only sibling, a brother three years older than me, was a Boy Scout. Often, during our Michigan summers, he would go with his troop on a camping trip. Sometimes my father would accompany the boys as they set up camp, made a fire using nothing but sticks, and caught their own dinner to roast.

During one of these excursions, my mother and I went along. Oh, we didn't rough it in the woods like the Boy Scouts did. We happily stayed in a small motel in the village of Kalkaska, Michigan, located in the upper portion of the Lower Peninsula. (Those of you who are not familiar with our Great Lakes State and its two peninsulas may need to locate a map to figure that one out!)

During our time in this quaint hamlet, we strolled the downtown streets window-shopping, ate at a local diner, and I swam in the outdoor pool while my mom sat on a wrought iron patio chair sipping her coffee.

Due to its many surrounding lakes and the Manistee River that runs nearby, Kalkaska is known for fishing. In fact, near the town center is a colossal statue of a brook trout. My mom took a picture of me standing next to this larger-than-life fish on that trip, and we recreated the pose when we went through the town again years later around my eighteenth birthday—long before recreating pictures was even a thing.

When my father and brother rejoined us once the Scouts had struck camp, we all hopped in our car and headed to a popular local attraction—a trout farm. For a small fee, you were given a fishing pole and some bait. You then stood on the dock to cast your line into the water in hopes of snagging a juicy trout to fry up for your supper. My brother went first. It took him about fifteen minutes, but he soon had a fish dangling off the end of his line.

Next came my turn. It seemed no sooner had I drawn back my fishing pole and flung my wrist forward to plunge the squirming, hooked worm into the water that I saw the red-and-white bobber dunk under the waves. Almost instantaneously, a nineteen-inch rainbow trout bit down on my line for his supper, not realizing that it was he who would soon be supper for me!

When I returned home from this mini vacation, I could hardly wait to tell my friends about my angling expedition and amazing catch. There was just one problem with my introduction to this outdoor pastime.

I thought that all fishing was this fast and fruitful.

The next time I tried fishing was with my uncle and cousins on a boat in the middle of a lake in upper Wisconsin. This experience was not at all like my first time. I baited my hook. (Okay. I sweet-talked my cousin Vicki into putting the worm on for me.) Then I tossed in my line, eager to once again see the bright red bobber dip its head underwater, indicating that a whopping fish had taken the bait—literally.

I waited. And I waited. A full thirty minutes or so passed before my bobber ever so slightly wiggled. But it must've been a fish that changed its mind. As the morning sun began to rise higher in the sky, my hopes for snagging a trout, a walleye, or even a tiny sunfish sank. This fishing trip was nothing like my experience at the trout farm. And it made me decide that I did not like this outdoor activity at all. When we returned to the cabin, I decided that for the rest of the vacation, my activities would center on swimming and suntanning rather than the boring, uneventful sport of fishing.

Just like my experience with fishing, our interactions in marriage can be disappointing directly due to our expectations based on what we experienced in the past.

You had a father who could fix anything that ever broke around the house. So you expect your spouse to also be a handy hubby.

Did your parents take time—no matter how worn-out they were—to clean up the kitchen each evening before going to bed? No wonder it frustrates the daylights out of you that the only thing your hubby wants to do every evening after dinner is kick back in the recliner and watch sports.

Were holidays and holy days a major production in your family growing up, with scads of aunts, uncles, cousins, and grandparents all descending upon your home, food in hand, to contribute to the meal? Well, that may be the reason for your bewilderment when your husband wants to celebrate at home with just you and the kids and expects you to make all seven courses of the holiday feast!

Expectations *often* come from past experience, but not *always*. They can also come from the present, especially from the assorted screens we stare at day after day. If we have developed the notion—based on unrealistic Hollywood depictions or seeing only half the story on social media—that success in marriage comes easy, we can grow discouraged.

See if any one of these "just like" lines of thought run through your brain:

- My husband should be attentive to my needs, even when I don't verbalize them out loud *just like* the husband in the movie my friends and I went to see last night.

- My marriage should include a weekly romantic dinner-out date, shared over the soft light of flickering candles, *just like* the picture my favorite lifestyle blogger posted tonight on Instagram.
- My husband should be a strong, spiritual presence in our home, taking very seriously teaching the children about God *just like* the author-husband of the website article I scrolled through while waiting at the doctor's office.
- My marriage should split the housework 50–50 *just like* I see my friend and her husband doing in a funny video they just posted on YouTube of the two of them cleaning out the garage.
- My man should buy me a large, sparkly, upgraded diamond ring, *just like* the one I see posted on my coworker's Facebook page rather than the tiny one he bought me decades ago.

These "just like" lines of thinking cause us to create unrealistic expectations and then usher in disappointment when these expectations are not met.

Both emotional baggage and our expectations cause the marital waters to become choppy, creating conflict and sometimes leading to arguments. But there is one more component to conflict that the Christian counselor mentioned when talking with the teens decades ago. I've seen this one rattle my contentment and cause me to pick a nasty fight now and then with my husband. This is the problem of "wrong perceptions."

THE PERCEPTION DECEPTION

Once I lived in a neighborhood with a man who could often be found outside in his front yard, tending to his gorgeous, vibrant flowerbeds. I enjoyed taking walks down the street where he lived, especially on a sunny day.

Being the chipper and gregarious sort, when I was out on my little strolls I would often smile and wave to any people I saw along the way. Or if someone's back was turned to me, I might shout out a cordial greeting such as, "Hi, neighbor!" or "Isn't this weather fantastic?" Since my fellow small-town folks are also friendly, I'd usually be met with a return greeting, or perhaps a short conversation would even commence. Then I'd go on my way and mosey back home.

I attempted to do this on several occasions with the flower-gardening man. Sometimes he would make eye contact with me, smile brightly, and wave back. But other times he would completely ignore me, even when I shouted out a good-natured greeting. I just couldn't figure it out. There was no rhyme or reason to this erratic behavior. I really didn't know the man beyond our occasional encounter, so I wondered why sometimes he seemed to be standoffish, ignoring me completely.

Boy, were my wrong perceptions kicking in big-time! I only learned this one day when chatting with a different neighbor, an elderly woman around the block. I mentioned the odd, sporadically social behavior of this man, asking if she knew why sometimes he refused to speak to—or even acknowledge—me. My question was met with a hearty chuckle. "Oh, Karen. You don't know?" "Know what?" I replied. "Mr. C. is completely deaf! If his back is turned to you or you aren't in his direct line of sight, he has no idea you're even around. He's not being rude. He just doesn't have a clue you're speaking to him."

I joined her in laughter and was thankful she had explained why he sometimes seemed to give me the cold shoulder. Now that I knew the facts, my wrong perception was shattered. What I thought to be true—I had a flower-loving but intermittently impolite neighbor—wasn't the case at all. He just couldn't hear me.

The textbook definition of a perception is a thought, opinion, or belief based on appearance. It might not be at all true in reality, but the person viewing the situation *believes* it to be. And because what we imagine to be true we declare to be true, we act on that incorrect assumption as if it were fact.

I may think my normally chatty and happy-go-lucky best friend is acting aloof and being rude by not returning my text messages. However, in reality, she may have just gotten some devastating news and is trying to process it before talking to me. I interpret her quiet demeanor and lack of responsiveness to my texts as cold and impolite. I form opinions in my mind, not based on what is *actually happening* in her life but on my *perception* of her behavior.

Perceptions creep into our marriage all the time. We survey our spouse's conduct and size up what we sense to be happening. Then because we don't dig deeper into the facts—and our brains interpret the perception as reality—we make our next move. Often, our reactive behavior takes our spouse completely by surprise. They know the reality of what's happening. What they don't know is our perception of the situation. Consequently, they may become not only bewildered but defensive as well. Then before we know it, an awful argument has broken out. Wrong perceptions are frequently a playground of turbulence in marriage.

THE 1–2–3 PUNCH

Any one component of this trio of trouble—emotional baggage, unmet expectations, or wrong perceptions—can cause or worsen conflict in your marriage. But sometimes all three of them are present, packing an awful 1–2–3 punch.

Let's say you and your dear husband are having a discussion about finances. It's the middle of April, and many bills are due before the calendar page gets flipped to May. Up until now, the two of you have been paying the bills in a rather haphazard way. Whenever one arrives in the mail, whoever happens to retrieve the mail that day assumes the task of paying the bill, either writing out a check and sending it off the old-fashioned way or hopping online to pay it from your bank account. You realize this method isn't working, and so both of you agree that it needs to be streamlined. Good starting point.

Now watch things go downhill.

When you begin the conversation about what needs to change, you can see right off the bat that the process is causing friction. You just can't seem to agree on *who* should be paying the bills, not to mention *how* they should be paid.

Your husband claims *you* should pay the bills, reasoning that you have more time in which to do so. "After all," he asserts, "you work *only* thirty hours per week and have just a five-minute commute to work." (He doesn't emphasize the word *only* when he speaks. However, you mentally—and heavily—highlight it when you hear him say the word. As if all the other words in that sentence are 12-point black font and the word *only* is not just three times the size but boldface and bright neon green!)

Your husband, on the other hand, puts in a full forty hours per week and makes a one-hour round-trip commute daily for his job as an IT guy. Your guy further states his opinion, proposing that you should set up online payments for the various bills you have as a couple. This suggested setup does not go over well with you. At. All.

Instead, you strongly feel this chore of marriage should be handled in an entirely different manner.

You suggest that both of you should share in the responsibility of this task. As the bills come in, they will be placed in your spare bedroom, where the computer is located and also where there's a desk with stamps in one of the drawers. You'll take turns monthly doing this chore, each person paying the bills however they'd like. You prefer a stamp and envelope. He would rather log on, tap away at the keys, and pay the bill online.

Your differing opinions lead to a tension-filled conversation. Each of you tries to convince the other that his or her way is the best way. You begin to nitpick at each other's chosen method, trying to shoot it down and prove it isn't the best approach. However, there's one thing you haven't taken into account: the terrible trio of baggage, expectations, and perceptions. Here's how these three culprits swirl together to create a perfect storm of conflict.

You have *baggage* in the area of finance. You were horrible at math as a high schooler. You stayed away from it in college when you obtained your associate's degree. And, fortunately, you only needed to take one basic math class, which you got through with the help of a tutor. You tried to pay a bill online once on a downloaded app on your phone. However, after spending more than twenty minutes trying, you just couldn't seem to figure it out. On top of all that, due to some comments your mother-in-law once made about your "little college degree," you've always felt as though you weren't as smart as your husband. You have an associate's degree; he has a master's.

Next, you and your man both have *expectations* when it comes to how this task should be handled. You grew up in a home where chores, including paying bills, were split 50–50. It was also not a very regimented home. Everyone kind of flew by the seat of their pants. Nevertheless, all the tasks eventually got done one way or another.

Your husband grew up in a home where the wife—a full-time homemaker—paid all the bills. His dad totally trusted his mom in that area, and she didn't seem to need or want any help.

This history sets up expectations for each of you. You expect the chore to be shared; he expects you to carry it all alone.

Finally, you have *perceptions*. He works with computers for a living. Doing things online is not only a big portion of his day, but it comes rather effortlessly to him. He's not intimidated by math. In fact, in his opinion, paying bills has nothing to do with math, because it's not actually performing any calculations but merely entering an amount and then hitting the send button on the keyboard. He perceives this as a relatively easy task, one the average person should be able to do.

Now rewind back to his "You work *only* thirty hours a week" remark. You perceive this statement of fact—and it *is* a fact—as your man implying that you aren't pulling as much weight financially as he is. However, he just sees it as a fact and nothing more. You log in ten hours less during the workweek than him. And you also spend about four fewer hours on the road than he does getting to and from your place of employment. He's just mentioning this because he thinks you have more time, that's all. But you interpret it as him thinking you have less ambition and aren't pulling your weight fiscally.

Now, each of you doesn't think consciously about pulling out your own baggage during this discussion. Your baggage has entwined itself into your brain's word processing program—the way you filter the sentences and phrases of others. If only you could peek into each other's suitcases, you might be able to better understand what the conflict centers around.

You see, your husband doesn't know that math seems daunting to you, or that you're intimidated by anything that even has numbers in it because your mind somehow views it as math. He's also not thinking about your family's loosey-goosey way of handling chores. He's not even aware that his mother made a cruel comment to you once about your associate's degree.

And although he knows you aren't a whiz at computers like him, the thought never crosses his mind that paying bills online or by using an app majorly stresses you out.

Meanwhile, you too are clueless of what your husband is dragging into the situation from his bygone days. You never knew his mom was in charge of the family finances, or that this reality plays into his proposition that you take on this particular household assignment.

If you as a couple can empty out the baggage, discuss each of your expectations, and separate the truth from the perceptions, perhaps you can come to an arrangement suitable to you both.

So, what's an exasperated spouse to do? Here are some ways the components of this terrible trio of trouble can be dealt with by heading them off at the pass.

Believe the best. Don't assume the worst. This phrase is one of the core values at the organization I write and speak for— Proverbs 31 Ministries. I've seen it prevent conflict and misunderstandings numerous times. It is also a great philosophy when interacting in marriage. Instead of always assuming the worst when your spouse says or does something, choose to believe the best of their intentions instead. Often, we assign a motive that is not at all true of someone, typically because of something that has happened in the past. We need to wipe the slate clean, not assuming anything but choosing to believe they sincerely have our best interests in mind.

How do we believe the best instead of assuming the worst? This leads us to our next spousal strategy.

Ask clarifying questions. Rather than jump to conclusions, ask questions. As you do, let your better half know what you *think* you hear them saying, and allow them to tell you if that is indeed what they really mean.

For example, think about the example above when we

imagined that your husband stated, "You work *only* thirty hours a week." Instead of assuming he is implying that you don't work as long and hard as he does, find out if that's truly what he meant. To do this, you could inquire, "What exactly is the point of you saying that I work *only* thirty hours a week? My heart highlighted the *only* part, and I took it as you saying I'm not pulling my weight financially because I don't work full-time like you. Is that what you meant?"

Now, I can't guarantee you will always be pleased with the answers to these questions. However, if you are misinterpreting language your spouse is using, by asking clarifying questions you can help dissipate tension in your communication. Then you won't be acting on an untrue premise, assigning a meaning to your husband's words he didn't intend. This also goes for the words typed out in texts—although a darling emoji or two can help convey the meaning of your words there: {winky face, red heart, thumbs up}

Describe your feelings while also recognizing that feelings aren't always based on facts. There is nothing wrong with mentioning how a conversation makes you feel. But understand that your feelings may not be based on the truth. If you have misunderstood what your spouse is saying or have assigned an incorrect motive to his words, your feelings may be unfounded. By all means, don't stuff your feelings inside. Do your best to describe the emotions you are experiencing in order to come to a greater understanding as you and your spouse work through the situation at hand.

Grant grace and don't give it an expiration date. Even during the times when you experience hurts due to something that your spouse says—or doesn't say—grant grace. Grace is a virtue that comes from God and shows love and mercy to someone, even when they don't deserve it. Grace is willing to forgive, to wipe the slate clean. We would do well to grant grace quickly and continually, knowing there will be times when we desperately need it as well. Grace creates space for our marriage to move forward rather than grow stagnant. So, grant grace. Over and over again.

FOR THE BIBLE TELLS ME SO

Have you ever noticed how some things in life are simple, but they're not at all easy?

For example, take mountain climbing. You just put one foot in front of the other, starting from the base of the mountain all the way to the tippy-top. Simple instructions, right? But this outdoor endeavor is definitely not easy.

Having a healthy marriage falls into the category of "simple but not easy." If we only interacted with our spouses the way the Bible instructs us to—and, in turn, our spouses did the same—we'd all have fewer skirmishes and squabbles. Instructions for marriage sound simple: "Just follow the Bible." But we all know from experience that doesn't make it easy.

However, when both spouses in a marriage treat each other in keeping with the directives of Scripture, they will experience fewer incidents of heated conflict.

Here are some Scripture verses that instruct us about how to build healthy, loving relationships. (You can also find them on page 215, designed as cards for you to photocopy and cut out, should you care to do so.) Pore over them. Ponder them. Even commit a few to memory. God's Word contains the best marital advice ever.

Ephesians 4:32: "Be kind and compassionate to one another, forgiving each other, just as in Christ God forgave you."

1 Peter 4:8: "Above all, love each other deeply, because love covers over a multitude of sins."

Romans 12:10: "Be devoted to one another in love. Honor one another above yourselves."

Ephesians 4:2–3: "Be completely humble and gentle; be patient, bearing with one another in love. Make every effort to keep the unity of the Spirit through the bond of peace."

Romans 13:8: "Let no debt remain outstanding, except the continuing debt to love one another, for whoever loves others has fulfilled the law."

And perhaps the simplest—but most relationship-altering—of all:

Luke 6:31: "Do to others as you would have them do to you."

DO YOU HAVE ANY CHIPS?

When my husband and I were first dating, I was mentored by one of my college professor's wives. She and her husband had a way to discuss daily if there was any lingering hurt or unresolved issues between them. They did this every night before going to bed. They'd take turns asking each other, "Do you have any chips?" Now I'm not talking about the potato or tortilla variety—although those can be a tasty bedtime snack. They meant a different kind of chip.

The wife told us the tale one night of how this regular ritual came to be. They explained it this way: marriage is like a fine, delicate porcelain teacup. It is lovely and useful, but it's also extremely breakable. A teacup is designed to hold a hot beverage. However, if there is even a slight chip or crack in the porcelain, when the boiling water is poured into the vessel, ready to steep a teabag, the weakened sides of the cup may suddenly shatter.

Your marriage mimics a fragile teacup. If you have little fractures and fissures in your relationship, due to unresolved tensions or misunderstandings from the emotional baggage, unmet expectations, or wrong perceptions either one of you has, your marriage won't be able to stand the heat of conflict. Instead, it may shatter, ending up with jagged pieces lying all around your feet.

However, if we are intentional to address the little nicks and cracks in our communication *before* they widen and grow any more serious, we can keep a healthy line of communication intact.

> *I love being married. It's so great to find one special person you want to annoy for the rest of your life.*
> *Rita Rudner*

Todd and I have adopted this same practice, though I wouldn't say we do it daily anymore. Yet there are still times we look at each other and ask, "Do you have any chips?" Because my husband is quite the jokester, he often makes some wisecrack about preferring barbecue over the sour-cream-and-onion variety. But sometimes the question opens up a much-needed discourse about something that transpired recently in our relationship. Making it a habit to truthfully and openly address these little cracks helps keep our marriage strong.

When cracks *are* discovered, honesty, apology, and pardon are often needed. Tend to your relationship early, before any minor damage magnifies and splits your marriage's harmony wide open and causes a fight. (Yes, of course, fights will still break out at times. But don't fret—fighting and feuding is what we will address next!)

Take time soon to discuss with your husband the trio of trouble that is emotional baggage, unmet expectations, and wrong perceptions. And then?

Keep loving. Keep learning. Keep asking for—and granting—forgiveness. Don't stop granting grace and wiping the slate clean. Keep the fresh cracks and crevices at bay daily.

Just keep showing up.

FOUR

Duel or Duet? Your Choice

Never go to bed mad. Stay up and fight.

PHYLLIS DILLER

"In your anger do not sin": Do not let the
sun go down while you are still angry,
and do not give the devil a foothold.

EPHESIANS 4:26–27

Marriage is a sticky situation. Oh, I don't mean the misunderstandings and miscommunications that come about organically when hammering out your days as husband and wife. I mean sticky as in glue.

Yes, glue.

I've heard marriage described in terms of a bottle of adhesive: two souls united—glued together if you will; attempting to pry them apart will cause great damage. In fact, my own husband spoke of superglue during the part of our ceremony where we recited the vows we wrote to each other. This is a great analogy . . . as long as the right adhesive is used.

Think of a glue stick. Perhaps even a fun and fancy one.

When I was substitute teaching in an elementary class, I once saw a brand that had bright, appealing packaging and whose glue was magically color-changing. It promised that its initial purple color would disappear, transforming to clear once the adhesive was set and the bond had become permanent. How cool!

But it didn't work. Not at all. Although the packaging was clever and flashy, and the promise seemed inviting, the adhesive was so poor it became unstuck easily, wrecking the projects and forcing the kids to scrap them and start over using a different kind of glue instead.

Contrast that with a handy type of adhesive we use regularly at our house called J-B Weld. Todd and I were once challenged to think of our marriage in terms of this useful substance.

J-B Weld is a hardware store product—an epoxy adhesive that can withstand extremely high temperatures, up to 600 degrees Fahrenheit. It's sold in a package with two tubes of adhesive that are entirely different materials. One is a hardener, and one is a resin. When equal amounts of both products are squeezed from the tube and then quickly mixed, a chemical reaction occurs. If the resulting mixture is placed on one object, it will bond a second object to it, creating a union that is strong and lasting. The bond isn't formed immediately, but over time—about six hours—it materializes.

J-B Weld can successfully be used on a multitude of surfaces including metal, glass, porcelain, wood, fabric, marble, and even paper. It's waterproof, chemical-resistant, and resists shock, vibration, and extreme temperature fluctuations.

We've used J-B Weld around our house to repair many broken items, including a stainless-steel colander I use weekly. About ten years ago, the bottom rim of the colander started to loosen and separate from the main part of the colander—the perforated bowl. If it were to come all the way off, the colander would be useless because it would no longer be able to balance on its own. However, with a little of this astonishing product, Todd mended it as good as new. Today, after a decade of use, Todd's repair on the colander shows no signs of coming loose—and my spaghetti noodles and freshly picked berries thank him.

I think that for many marriages, we first get attracted by our spouse's pretty packaging. We entertain fun thoughts of being married and the promise of excitement and contentment we think no longer being single will bring. That's right—like the glue stick. We enter into our nuptials believing our relationship will be full of singing birds, patches of posies, and cotton-candy clouds. Then along comes the clashes of will, the kerfuffles and fights, even the wear-and-tear of everyday life. When such events materialize, we don't have a strong bond to hold us together. The stickiness was only temporary, the adhesive ineffective. There is very little union left.

But that is not the picture of a lasting marriage. A marriage that keeps showing up and going the distance is so much more like J-B Weld.

When a husband and wife are joined together in holy matrimony, you have two people who, in substance, are not at all alike. They begin to interact as spouses. Some of the exchanges are enjoyable. Others are . . . not so much. Over time, when each not-like-the-other individual equally pours out their hearts, their thoughts, even their annoyances with each other, something happens. Difficult discussions. And friction. Minor frustration and major fights. But through the intensity of the interactions between the two, over time a strong bond is formed. The heat of conflict—when mixed with forgiveness and grace—can bond two distinct individuals into a rock-solid, united team.

Over the years, Todd and I have disagreed about numerous issues. (We just had a tiff ten minutes ago!) Our first few years of marriage even included me sometimes creating conflict where none existed because I like a good fight now and then—to debate and prove I'm right. Thankfully, a mentor noticed this in me and kindly suggested I cut it out before it totally ruined my marriage.

Todd and I have used slightly salty (me) or even sarcastic (Todd) words when voicing our differences. We've had H-U-G-E verbal brawls over issues of parenting. (I like to step in and prevent a child's wrong choice; he prefers to step back and let them make it, suffer the consequences, and learn the hard lesson.)

We've had to talk and talk, and then talk some more. Explain. Give examples. Ask for input from others when we couldn't agree. We've had to learn to shut our mouths long enough to actually *listen* to the other person's thoughts and try to comprehend their views. (Okay—not so much Todd, but me. He struggles with the opposite—speaking his mind; you know, once he's actually decided and can verbalize what he really thinks. This process can sometimes take up to three days. Do you even *know* how long three days can seem when a verbal processor like me has to hold my tongue and not talk about it?)

> *All men make mistakes, but married men find out about them sooner.*
> Red Skelton

But even though these heated interactions seem like they may be detrimental, they aren't. Something happens when two very opposite people get all mixed up in the normal skirmishes that are sure to come in marriage. Sure, the clashes get intense. But you also get stronger! Learning to work through differences and handle conflict in a healthy way allows your bond to solidify and hold. It doesn't always get easier, but you learn to hang in there and face the heat together.

Your love learns to last.

No slightly tacky, cheap fixes endure, but a relationship that withstands the heat of interaction, by dealing with it properly, becomes shatterproof over time. Determine to see conflict— even arguments—as good. When there is a healthy resolution, you gain a greater understanding of each other. And you reconcile in a manner that strengthens your relationship.

TROUBLE IN PARADISE

Having a successful marriage is hard. (Remember our premises from chapter 1—"*marriage is hard* and *it's not about me*"?) It's easier to let your relationship disintegrate and become characterized by domestic duels than it is to put in the sweat and tears required to have your relationship become a melodious duet— with each spouse playing their part. These parts are separate from, but in harmony with, the other. It takes a great amount of resolve, focus, and, yes, even work for a marital duet to be sung in tune. Before we step up to the mic, we have to first stop expecting a trouble-free, walk-in-the-park marriage. There *will* be trouble. Let's get equipped and ready to stare it straight in the face and deal with it.

Speaking of trouble . . .

In John 16, we find Jesus speaking with his disciples before his crucifixion, trying to prepare them for what is to come in the days ahead. It's also a great portion of Scripture for us to read today, especially when we face trying times.

One particular verse that springs off the page for me is verse 33. Jesus says, "I have told you these things, so that in me you may have peace. In this world you will have trouble. But take heart! I have overcome the world."

Did you catch it? Jesus himself tells us that in this world we will have trouble. Not *might* have trouble—*will* have trouble. Count on it. Jesus said it. *So why, then*, I wonder, *am I always so surprised when it comes?* At such times, I exasperatingly ask the question, "Why?"

Wrong question.

If you too blink with surprise at trouble, let's adopt the habit of asking ourselves a different question. Not "why?" but "so what?" And I don't mean that in a flippant, dismissive way. I mean sincerely inquiring, "*So what* do I do now? How do I respond?"

The answers to those two queries are not always the same, of course, but one thing should always be consistent: we need to know that in this life we will have trouble. Let's expect it, not shrink away from it. Let's meet it head-on. How do we do this? The answer is also found in John 16:33. Read it again: "I have told you these things, so that in me you may have peace. In this world you will have trouble. But take heart! *I have overcome the world*" (emphasis mine).

Take heart. Christ has already overcome.

Our answer is found in Christ. In knowing him. Spending time with him, face in our Bibles and hearts open to his truth. In allowing him to chisel away the hardness in our hearts by way of our sandpaper spouses. And yes, even through our spats and emotional scuffles. Jesus can teach us how to communicate, how to resist getting historical. How to lean in and really listen (preachin' to myself on that one). How to overlook an offense. And how to forgive.

Yes, Christ is the solution. Always. Every time. Submerge yourself in Scripture, expecting that those times of trouble will come. Something incredible happens when we adjust our attitude, switching our thinking from *Why is this happening to me?* to *I know that trouble comes with the territory. So what do I do* this time, *Jesus?*

Trouble in paradise materializes in many forms. I surveyed

my followers on social media recently to discover what they thought were the greatest areas of difficulty in married life. I found the results to be a mix of what I expected and some rather surprising insights.

Just over a thousand women took the poll. I asked them to check as many boxes as they wanted that represented an area where they encountered tension in their marriage, including dealing with the in-laws, sharing the workload around the house, and trust issues.

Of the thousand wives, here's the percentage who struggle in each of the areas that ended up comprising the top five:

- communication: 67 percent
- finances: 52 percent
- parenting the kids: 37 percent
- competing with technology for attention: 36 percent
- horizontal friendliness (sex!): 36 percent

I also allowed them to check a box that read "other" and then to list their own area of conflict in marriage not given as a choice in the survey. Here are some of those responses:

- a workaholic spouse
- family busyness
- blended family issues
- caring for aging parents
- being at different levels of interest in spiritual matters
- and, overwhelmingly, dealing with a husband who has gotten caught—or admitted to—looking at porn

There is no way even the wisest of trained counselors can give solutions to these various trials of marriage on the pages of just one book. *My* main aim is simply to provide some tools to help you work through conflict, in keeping with Scripture, no matter what the conflict is. And I list these common issues of concern to help you see that you are not alone.

You're not alone because you have sisters who also struggle, and you're not alone because you have a Savior who—being miraculously and mysteriously fully God *and* fully man—also struggled while here on earth.

Hebrews 4:15–16 is a gift to us in this area. It states:

> For we do not have a high priest who is unable to empathize with our weaknesses, but we have one who has been tempted in every way, just as we are—yet he did not sin. Let us then approach God's throne of grace with confidence, so that we may receive mercy and find grace to help us in our time of need.

Listen to me, friends—I *cling* to this verse often and the many rich realities it contains.

Jesus empathizes with us. He was tempted in *every* way—just like we are! However, he didn't give in to temptation. He declined to sin. So, we can go to God—our King—boldly and with assurance. He rules with *grace*—a multifaceted biblical concept that means "undeserved favor in the eyes of the Lord." It is also descriptive, denoting a superior who bends or stoops to show kindness to an inferior, such as a king lowering himself to assist a servant.

God will give us this grace and also grant mercy—inexhaustible compassion and love—right when we most need it.

So, when we are tempted in every way—tempted to give up trying to have healthy communication, tempted to storm away in anger, tempted to point out our spouse's non-strengths and boast about our own brilliant ideas, tempted to lash out and hurl hate—Jesus gets us. He understands! Run to him. Throw yourself at the foot of the cross and cry out to him for help.

He will meet you every time.

BATTLE PREVENTION

Now, I am undoubtedly no licensed counselor. My formal education is limited to having an undergraduate degree in social science. However, after three decades of marriage, I've discovered some methods for dealing with conflict that I hope to share with you here. And I believe that when these approaches are applied to any of the above areas—or even your own unique challenges—they can be helpful.

However, let me just stop now and once again urge that if you are dealing with a serious issue such as adultery or porn, or if the conflict you experience about any of the issues causes arguments that escalate to the point that they frighten you due to verbal abuse or physical harm, get help! Reach out to your pastor if you have one. Find a Christian counselor in your area by visiting ccn.thedirectorywidget.com. Or if you are being abused, *please* call the National Domestic Abuse Hotline at 1-800-799-7233 or visit www.thehotline.org.

Before we explore what to do when conflict arises, let's talk a bit about preventing it from happening in the first place. Doesn't that make much more sense? I mean, who wants to spend all kinds of time out in the yard with a screwdriver, popping out dandelions that have poked their bright yellow heads through the lush, green grass? Wouldn't it be easier to sprinkle on a little organic weed-and-feed, preventing their appearance instead?

You can do the same with the areas of marriage where you and your spouse constantly seem to hop on the struggle bus.

Rather than having to stop and deal once again with an area of conflict, try a smidgeon of prevention instead.

We've already discussed step number one—expecting trouble. We're going to stop freaking out when it rings the doorbell. It's gonna come calling. Next step . . .

You know best both your relationship and your repeated hot buttons, so you'll want to make sure you address those unique characteristics when you and your husband talk. I'm just giving some ideas to help get you started, to prime the pump, and to encourage you to lay down a healthy framework from which to begin.

The following guidelines, when implemented, may prevent a squabble from breaking out. I'm also certain you can come up with some others yourself. (And by that, I don't mean you coming up with them and then barking them out to your husband. I mean the *two of you*, sitting down, maybe enjoying your favorite beverage, and hammering out ideas that work especially for you.)

1. When something even slightly begins to bother us, we will bring it up to the other person before it has had time to fester and grow.

2. We will not discuss issues when one or both of us is headed out the door somewhere.

3. We will not discuss issues when one of us is overly tired and needs to go to bed.

4. We will set a regular time each week (or every few days) to ask if either of us is feeling offended by anything. (Revisit "Do You Have Any Chips?" on page 74 to see how Todd and I do this.)

5. We will learn to ask each other "What do you need from me this week?" in order to clarify our expectations and not assume our spouse knows what we expect from them in our relationship, around the house, or with the kids.

6. We will commit to pray about avoiding unhealthy and unproductive fights in our marriage when at all possible. We will ask God to help us do four things: communicate effectively, not drag our baggage into discussions, lower our expectations, and have accurate perceptions.

Are there any other guidelines you and your husband can think of that might help squelch a squabble before it breaks out?

RULES OF ENGAGEMENT (THAT YOU PROBABLY NEVER TALKED ABOUT DURING YOUR ENGAGEMENT!)

Even with the utmost effort to stop a skirmish before it breaks out, there will be times you need to discuss sensitive topics—topics that can lead to a clash. At those times we need to watch our words and actions carefully, making sure they don't throw fuel on any kindling that may be present. And—also true—if one or both spouses tend to be a stuffer, cramming away their emotions rather than talking about them, they'll need to learn to speak up and speak honestly.

For me, stuffing isn't usually an issue. Quite the opposite. My mouth often runs ahead of my brain. At these times, my words can get me in a tangled-up mess when interacting with my husband.

My husband, on the other hand, is content to keep his feelings inside, preferring to just bury them and hope they go away rather than take the time and effort to hash things over, knowing a fight may ensue otherwise.

You've heard of the old "fight or flight" response to danger or conflict? Well, I go for option A—fight. But Todd looks for the first flight outta here! This is one of the dynamics of our relationship that drives both of us the most crazy. If not careful and calculated, here is the plot that plays out:

A situation rears its head. It can be anything. Let's say it's something with one of the children, but you can easily fill in your own blank, as almost any potentially discord-producing situation will work. At any rate, it happens. And then it's off to the races we go.

I get ticked off. So does he. However, my level of ticked seems to be several notches higher because I think fast and then verbalize my displeasure instantaneously—you know, with lots of "What were you thinking?" and "I can't believe you did that!"'s thrown in for added effect. I want to discuss the situation right then and there.

My dear husband, not being the verbal processor that I am, wants to go away. Far away. He wants to have time to think about things thoroughly before getting into a discussion. And so he says nothing. *Nada!* In fact, he usually wanders off and finds something productive to do quietly, like tidy up the garage or go pull some weeds. (Why I don't just happily let him go do these things makes absolutely no sense. I really should rethink my "Gotta discuss this right now!" ways and wait until he finishes up the project!)

Where was I? Oh yeah. I want to deal with it—right now and out loud. He wants to mull things over before speaking, to make sure he really knows what he thinks.

He wants to back away. I prefer to back him into a corner.
I burst out. He shuts down.
I accuse. He defends and justifies.
Then he accuses, and *I* defend and justify.
He zigs. I zag.
Repeat to infinity.

All the while, we are spinning our relational wheels, going basically nowhere. Well, except over ground we've covered a gazillion times in our marriage.

We call it "file 13."

This is the phrase we use to paint a word picture of what we tend to do in our dialogue during disputes. You know how often the issue *isn't really* the issue. It isn't what just happened with how one of us handled a situation with one of the kids (or more often, how I complain that he *didn't* handle a situation when he should have!). It is the same issue—file 13—that bubbles to the surface. We delve into the filing cabinet of our minds and pull the same old tattered manila folder out again. What is the issue in file 13?

File 13 is how we communicate—or don't—during conflict.

He is an escaper who avoids. I am a confronter who attacks. This is at the crux of so many of our communication issues that I lost count the first few weeks of our marriage. It often comes out in the words we say to each other when we *do* enter into discussion, each accusing the other one of bad behavior. The person who wants to verbally process the situation right away views the other as uncooperative for not doing so. The one who wants to have a cooling-off period and think through things before opening a conversation views their spouse as combative.

I even find that these different ways of handling issues have surfaced when we critique each other's parenting. I accuse him of avoiding issues, sweeping them under the rug without addressing them. He thinks I stir up issues verbally by provoking the kids with dozens of questions—many of them glazed with subtle hints of distrust and accusation. And you know what? There is some truth in both of these views.

What we have here is a beyond-exasperated couple—tired of pulling out file 13 and walloping each other upside the head emotionally. When this happens, what can an almost-over-the-edge couple do?

Fight fair and behave like Jesus.

Having a Christian marriage doesn't mean everything is all peachy all the time. We are going to disagree. We are going to verbally battle and brawl. The difference is in learning to discuss things in a civil manner with the goal of resolving the conflict—and of reconciling if your relationship has been damaged.

Fight fair and behave like Jesus.

I love what Pastor Scott Sauls posted on his Twitter account recently, which he graciously said I could share with you. This treasure of a Tweet sums up the two wrong ways of dealing with conflict that are often displayed in marriage, but it also shows us a better way. It goes like this:

> Avoiding conflict = Cowardice
> Savoring conflict = Aggression
> Redeeming conflict = Christian[1]

Yes! That's it! Don't avoid. Don't savor. Run to the Savior and redeem instead.

We can learn to work through conflict, restoring our relationship and choosing to view the heat of conflict as good—*J-B Weld-style good*—if it causes our love to grow stronger. We can choose to live out the plan of redemption by apologizing, forgiving, and forging onward—hand in hand and hearts intact.

You with me? Good. Now just how do we do this?

Here are some "fighting fair" rules of engagement that may help. Again, discuss these with your spouse and also take a crack at coming up with any of your own to add to the mix.

We will refrain from using superlatives. When discussing issues, we pledge to refrain from using superlatives such as "you always . . ." or "you never . . ." and will only talk about the incident at hand, treating it as its own matter. Superlatives are often exaggerations. They put our spouse on the defense right away. When they do, all of a sudden, our beloved is reacting to the fact that we painted him in a light that asserts he is regularly in the wrong. He then launches into a rebuttal of this assertion. Then the conversation gets way off track, failing to address the issue at hand. So, make a commitment to never say "never"!

Next helpful guideline . . .

We will refrain from getting historical. Okay—confession time. I so stink at this! When Todd and I fight, I have a habit of dredging up the past. And I'll bet some of you reading this also do it. At least sometimes. You pull out your own "file 13"—that issue you visit repeatedly but never solve. Stop it already. Leave the past in the past—which becomes easier the more we deal with conflict in a healthy manner by not leaving hurts unaddressed or loose ends of forgiveness untied.

We will try to express how we feel. When we have a disagreement, we try to frame the discussion by expressing how *we* feel rather than hyperfocusing on the other person's words or actions. This guideline helps us take ownership. Its goal is to describe our feelings in a way that our spouse can understand. And it also allows our partner to drop any defensive attitude *they* may have, because they won't feel like their actions are being attacked. So, for example, you might say, "When you do A, I feel B."

We will stick to the facts. When we do mention our spouse's words or actions, we will truthfully state the facts without hitching descriptive adjectives to it. For example, simply stating, "When you didn't introduce me to your friend from high school when we saw him at the bank . . ." instead of the more colorful "when you were utterly obnoxious the other day and so rudely neglected to introduce me to your friend from high school when we saw him at the bank . . ." (More confession: I can come up with descriptive adjectives that put my husband in the most dreadful light. Adjectives. All. Day. Long.)

We will not assign a motive. We pledge to not assign motives to our spouse's words or actions, taking personally that which was not meant to be personal. And when a spouse is simply stating facts, we won't read more into it, taking it to heart and erroneously assuming they meant something derogatory. For example, we won't say, "You think I'm incompetent and forgetful!" when your husband asks if you remembered to swing by the car dealership, as he asked, to grab the tube of touch-up paint he ordered for the ding on your vehicle. Nope. He's just ready to cover over the ding, and so he needs the paint to do so. That's all.

We will agree to disagree. You will not always agree on everything. Accept this fact now. So, what do you do when you don't agree on how to handle a situation in your family?

Next!

We will speak the truth—lovingly. We find this concept of speaking the truth in love in Ephesians 4:15. Depending on our personalities, we tend to focus more on just one half of that verse to the neglect of the other. Either we blurt out the truth in a not-so-loving fashion or we reason the only loving way to proceed is not to utter a word. Tell the truth. But be loving while doing it. Real love flourishes best when it is rooted in the earth of honesty.

We will seek to find common ground. Those trained to negotiate—whether in business, the military, or relationally—know that the first step when negotiating is to find common ground. Maybe you can't concur on what action to take, but striving to find common ground—such as the reason you want to resolve the conflict—helps defuse tempers and sets you on the path to resolution.

We will learn and practice the fine art of compromise. Yes, compromise—the definition of which good ole Webster's dictionary says is "a settlement of differences by arbitration or by consent reached by mutual concessions." So, give in a little to get along. Not in matters of serious importance and certainly not in matters of sin, but in the other things? Yes. Give in a little. *Both* of you.

We will remember that our spouse is not the enemy. When we go head-to-head in a spat, we're viewing each other as the enemy. We have to remember who the *real* enemy of marriage is—Satan. He seeks to steal, kill, and destroy (John 10:10). Todd and I often remind ourselves of this by saying out loud, "You are not my enemy." Stand side by side, fighting *for* your marriage, rather than going toe-to-toe, fighting *in* it.

We will pray through. I've had older mentors in my life talk about this concept. Rather than praying *about* something, pray *through* it. Seek Scripture. Keep the lines of communication open. When both of you are earnestly pursuing God's solution to a problem—and you refuse to stop self-seeking—God will be faithful to give the answer.

We will allow space to let God work. Your spouse doesn't need two Holy Spirits. Back off. Be quiet. Talk only to God—and maybe to one trusted friend. (More about this in chapter 8.) Keep in mind what the late Billy Graham said: "It is the Holy Spirit's job to convict, God's job to judge, and my job to love."[2]

We will be a couple who apologizes to—and also forgives— each other. This is the secret! Keep showing up, ready to forgive. Even the best marriages sometimes have clashes of will. If we think our relationships will be void of domestic duels for the rest of our lives—if only we try hard enough—we are fooling ourselves. The frequency will decrease. You will head off more arguments at the pass. However, they will still occur sometimes. When they do, it's imperative that you properly resolve the issue, make up, and move on. I'd venture to guess that most of us would claim to know the importance of forgiveness. However, I have a sneaking suspicion that we also identify with an author and theologian by the name of Clive (better known as C. S.) Lewis. He correctly observed, "Everyone says forgiveness is a lovely idea, until they have something to forgive."[3] How true!

The concept of forgiveness seems lofty and lovely, and we love to read stories about it, whether in ancient Scripture or in current culture right there on the screens of our devices. But when we ourselves have been personally wronged, a root of bitterness can begin to grow in our hearts, making us adverse to the idea of forgiving. But when we choose to forgive—often and early—we hit the reset button on our relationship, wiping the slate clean. No keeping score of the other person's wrongs. Or as I once heard said, "Forgiveness is not about keeping score but about losing count." A weathered, wooden sign in one of my favorite local artisan shops echoes this. Its stenciled words announce, "The first to apologize is the bravest. The first to forgive is the strongest. The first to forget is the happiest."

REDUCING THE RECOVERY TIME

I opened the door to the bookstore and quickly walked to the cafe near the back of the building. It was release day for one of my books, and I was getting ready to greet dozens of people for a book signing—smile on face and pen in place.

My team and I made sure we had tasty treats and plenty of hot coffee for my readers to enjoy that night. They came to celebrate the book's birth, hear a short presentation from me, and then partake in an open question-and-answer time. A few of my close friends came out for the night, including my friend Cindy. Always the cheerleader and rarely without confetti to throw—I'm talking literal confetti; it's her trademark, and she's known for chucking it at a moment's notice—she had encouraging words to say about my book. However, it was something else she said to me at the end of the night that nearly stopped me in my tracks.

"Oh, Karen. I just love the spark that I see between you and Todd. You can tell from the look in your eyes when you speak to one another that you are just so in love. I even see it when you look at each other from across the room." I smiled and thanked her as I grabbed another cup of coffee and headed back to my book-signing stool. However, everything in me wanted to shout, "Are you kidding me right now? I don't know what's in your mug, lady, but you are sorely mistaken!"

Little did sweet Cindy know that Todd and I had just had a major tiff in the car on the way to the release party. What began as my husband offering to do a favor for me on a busy day ended up with me rather upset over his choice of paper products on which to serve the refreshments to said guests—many of whom had traveled from afar.

I envisioned something kinda cute—maybe with a decorative flair or at least a hint of color. Yes, some darling small dessert plates that just screamed adorable. Mr. Frugal-and-Function thought only of utility and price. We needed plates to hold snacks. That is all. Well, obviously you know where this train is headed—his big-box-store selection, while cost-effective, simply did not measure up to my standards. He chose the jumbo-sized, stark-white paper plates.

I unloaded on him, vocalizing my displeasure, using superlatives, and getting very historical. (Yes, I failed to take my own advice when met with such social tragedies such as plain white plates at a book release gala.)

However, the Holy Spirit—as he often does—tapped me on the heart, prompting me to drop it already and respectfully apologize. Thankfully, I did.

I said I was sorry. He forgave me. We grabbed the hideous . . . *um* . . . the adequate paper products (that nobody in attendance that night even remembers today), and we went into the book release party with no chips in our teacups or offenses between us.

The sparks that flew in our fight quickly dissipated, and the spark in our eyes for each other returned. Then Cindy saw it.

Please know that I don't tell you this story to brag about how wonderfully I apologize and reconcile with my husband. (Because, honey, it ain't always the case!) But I'm getting a little close to word count on this chapter, so I won't tell of those other times right now. ;-) I tell it to you because *it has not always been this way.*

There have been times in my marriage when something trivial like this would've made me upset with my husband for days. But I've discovered that it's just not worth it. In fact, I often pose questions to myself to discover if it's really worth the turmoil and tension that ensue when I make a mountain out of a moment—a moment when my husband has a faux pas or does something a different way than I would.

Questions such as . . .

- In light of the negative feelings it will cause at this precise moment, is it worth it?
- In light of the tension this will bring to our atmosphere for the rest of today, is it worth it?
- In light of eternity, is it worth it?

The answer is usually nope—three times over.

A huge part of learning to let things roll off our backs comes when we keep in mind what we read in Romans 8:5–6: "Those who live according to the flesh have their minds set on what the flesh desires; but those who live in accordance with the Spirit have their minds set on what the Spirit desires. The mind governed by the flesh is death, but the mind governed by the Spirit is life and peace."

We have a choice when it comes to our behavior, especially when responding to our spouse during conflict. We can let our mind be governed by the Spirit. Or we can let it be controlled by the flesh. My husband calls the latter "throwing flesh balls," meaning not caring at all what the Spirit says but reaching deep into our arsenal of ugly and then whipping a verbal ball of unflattering irritation at our spouse.

> *Don't hang up on your marriage. Hang in there instead.*

But look back at what is promised when we set our minds on what the Spirit desires! We are told we will have a mind governed by life and peace. Don't those two words just draw you in?

Life.

Peace.

Wouldn't you love to have these words be characteristic of your marriage—a relationship that is way more duet than duel?

When the conflict comes—and it most certainly will—remember this:

Every new day is an *exercise in*—and *excuse to*—love. To forgive. To never stop starting over again.

Don't hang up on your marriage. Hang in there instead.

Just keep showing up.

PROVERBS

POWER VERSES FOR QUARREL PREVENTION AND REDUCTION

The suggestions in this chapter are helpful to keep in mind, but perhaps our most critical tool is Scripture memory. Memorize these pithy proverbs, keeping them in mind when you want to avoid quarrels.

Proverbs 15:18: "A hot-tempered person stirs up conflict, but the one who is patient calms a quarrel."

Proverbs 17:14: "Starting a quarrel is like breaching a dam; so drop the matter before a dispute breaks out."

Proverbs 17:19: "Whoever loves a quarrel loves sin; whoever builds a high gate invites destruction."

Proverbs 18:1: "An unfriendly person pursues selfish ends and against all sound judgment starts quarrels."

Proverbs 18:13: "To answer before listening—that is folly and shame."

Proverbs 20:3: "It is to one's honor to avoid strife, but every fool is quick to quarrel."

Proverbs 22:10: "Drive out the mocker, and out goes strife; quarrels and insults are ended."

Proverbs 26:21: "As charcoal to embers and as wood to fire, so is a quarrelsome person for kindling strife."

And then my personal favorites—all having to do with a nagging or quarrelsome wife.

Proverbs 21:9: "Better to live on a corner of the roof than share a house with a quarrelsome wife."*

Also see Proverbs 25:24, where again dwelling in a crammed corner is preferred over being roomies with a not-so-sweet sweetheart.

Proverbs 21:19: "Better to live in a desert than with a quarrelsome and nagging wife."

Proverbs 27:15: "A quarrelsome wife is like the dripping of a leaky roof in a rainstorm."*

Oh, boy! Does that last one ever bring back funny memories! When we were first married, we hung around a couple from our Bible study with whom we shared a private joke. When either of us wives began to nag or badger about something, one of the husbands would just ever so quietly—and in a staccato, rhythmic way—begin to whisper under his breath, "Drip. Drip. Drip." It didn't make us mad. It made us laugh as we realized what we actually sounded like. (And don't worry, when the husbands started getting cantankerous, we also had a method to alert them to their behavior. We only needed to shoot them "the look," and they got the message!)

FIVE

You've Lost That Lovin' Feelin'

*Love God and he will enable you to love
others even when they disappoint you.*
FRANCINE RIVERS

Love never fails.
1 CORINTHIANS 13:8

Isn't it the sweetest thing to spot a young couple who appear intoxicated with love? Maybe that couple at the table beside you at the cozy, off-the-beaten-path coffee shop. The way they look into each other's eyes dreamily. Their slight and constant smiles warmly washing across their faces give indication that they've waited with anticipation for the chance to spend some time together. And the lovely chamber music playing softly over the sound system perfectly fits the scene.

I watched one such couple recently when I was spending time at a local café, slowly nursing a grande coconut latte while trying to edit a chapter of this book. (Okay, and while sometimes also watching the latest blooper videos being shared on social media for a little brain break!) What struck me most was the way the young lovers were on their best interpersonal behavior.

They spoke kindly to each other. (Yes, I eavesdropped. I couldn't help it—the café was tiny, and their voices were easily heard.) Their words had not a hint of frustration for the entire hour and a half they sat there, slowly sipping their own tasty coffee concoctions. In fact, I never sensed even a second of boredom as they interacted. They were hyperfocused on each other.

My brain couldn't help but contrast them with another couple my husband and I sat near when we went out for lunch on a Saturday afternoon the week prior. We were dining at a quaint grill a few towns away, a place we first discovered when we bought a dinner-for-two Groupon while only paying the price of one. (We go "Groupon dating" often. We are all highfalutin' like that. Okay. Actually, we're just cheap!) This couple, probably in their midthirties, looked as though they would rather be scrubbing out garbage cans than spending time with each other that day.

At first, they just seemed bored, each of them looking at their phones or staring off into the distance. But soon they exchanged cross words, giving only a halfhearted attempt to keep them under their breath. The exchange made us realize that something must've happened prior to their outing that caused them to be totally ticked off at each other.

Their irritation wasn't easily disguised, although they did seem to notice when their volume was escalating, so they'd try to crank it down a decibel or two. Once their food arrived, they stopped fighting. But they also stopped talking. They barely even made eye contact as they ate. I sure hoped they too had gotten their dinners at a discount. It'd be a crying shame to pay full price for their *un*-happy meals. (← See what I did right there?)

When it was time to leave, the woman—whom we assumed

from the wedding ring on her finger was his wife—grabbed her coat and headed out of the restaurant first. The man slapped down some cash, put on his jacket, and followed—their meal of misery now over.

I'm sure all of us have experienced times when we were frustrated with our spouses but still had to be in public for some reason. And it's what might have happened to this cantankerous couple that day. Yet I tend to observe kind and affectionate actions from young millennial couples, but more often bouts of boredom—or even of battles—from the middle-aged and older crowd. I wouldn't say always, but usually.

My wife tells me that if I ever decide to leave, she is coming with me.

Jon Bon Jovi

In fact, my husband and I like to play a little game when we take our middle-aged selves out on the town. We call it "Married or Matched?" It goes like this: a man and woman are out munching on sub sandwiches. Or splitting a pizza. Or sitting beside one another waiting for the movie previews to start. We try to guess from their behavior whether they are married or whether they were just recently matched on an online dating site and are on their first date.

Of course, sometimes the presence or absence of wedding rings might give it away. However, we sadly observe a stark contrast between couples who are wearing the rings and those who are not. Often the "are not" couples appear attentive and interested in what each other is saying. And often the married ones appear as though they're not on a date with their darling but instead are on hour three of sitting in an orthodontist's waiting room—bored out of their ever-lovin' minds.

Our little guessing game also has led to a goal in our marriage. We hope that when people see us interacting in public, they'll think we're on our first date! I'm not saying that we suddenly morph into actors, trying to put on a show for whomever may be watching (or eavesdropping) on us. But we try to earnestly pay attention to each other's words. To genuinely enjoy each other's company. To speak kindly. To be grateful for the time we can spend together as husband and wife, splitting our deeply discounted meal or sipping a steamy and creamy hot beverage at our local coffee shop—most likely also purchased with a BOGO coupon.

So, why don't some couples who've been married a few years—or even several decades—seem to display obvious affection for each other? What happened to love?

WHERE IS THE LOVE?

Todd and I met when I was nineteen and he was twenty. We lived in the same campus dormitory but in different wings. Our countryside college was so small that residents of all three dorms ate their meals together in another building across campus where the common dining hall was located. Due to this setup—and the fact that we had a few of the same classes—we had lots of time to spend together, which we most certainly did during the first year we met. Then it came time to have our little DTR talk—define the relationship—and we officially became an item and, a year after that, engaged.

College life was rather monotonous. Get up. Go to class. Sit through chapel. Go to more classes. Write a paper. Eat meals. Occasionally make the twenty-minute drive into the city to eat out or take in a movie. (There was only a bank, a gas station, and a corner pharmacy within walking distance of campus.)

Although our schedules and schooling lacked pizzazz, the time of our dating relationship was full of elation and interest.

When I was with Todd, I was "in my glory," as my roommate referred to it. When I wasn't with him, I was incessantly thinking about my beau and anticipating the next time we would be together, even though our love story was playing out before the backdrop of the repetitive routine of college life.

Todd and I showed our thoughts about, and care for, each other in little ways. He'd have someone on my all-girls/no-males-allowed floor slip me a greeting card under my door. When I did need to drive into the city, I'd return with a to-go double-dip dish of his favorite ice cream—pistachio—from a retro ice cream parlor near the mall. I'd save him a seat in philosophy class. He'd go up and refill my beverage at dinner. We'd take a walk around town and talk about everything—or about nothing. Mostly, we deeply drank in the love that was evident in our interactions, smack-dab in the center of our ordinary days.

Our rather routine life did not at all hinder our enthusiasm about our relationship.

Fast-forward a few decades in the life of a married couple. Life is also rather routine. Get up. Go to work. Pay bills. Perform chores. Get groceries. Watch the kiddos do all the things kiddos do. Eat meals. Go to bed. Same song, new verse. But it seems that somehow, we don't find it as easy to rise above the routine and see sparks in our love anymore. In fact, often couples who've been married a while have a love that is more fizzle than sizzle. Why?

Because when met with the routine and repetitiveness of life, our relationships may follow suit—becoming rather perfunctory themselves. Familiarity doesn't just have the potential to breed contempt; it also can bring about boredom.

Our dating days were characterized by newness. Isn't it easy to get excited about something brand-new? I love to discover new towns while traveling, to buy a cozy new sweater to wear on a chilly fall day. Why, I even get slightly giddy over a brand-spanking-new kitchen towel or toothbrush! So it doesn't surprise me that our minds go in search of something new when they feel stuck in a state of monotony.

But maybe the solution isn't to look outward, grabbing hold of something fresh and unfamiliar. Perhaps the solution comes by looking at our same old same old with fresh eyes. When we do, we may just discover a little magic in the mundane.

THAT LOVIN' FEELIN'

One day we wake up and realize that The Righteous Brothers were right when they crooned, "You've lost that lovin' feelin' . . . now it's gone, gone, gone." How do we go backward and regain the ushy-gushy feelings we had toward each other? There has to be a way, right?

Um . . . not really. In my opinion, we can't go back and have those exact same feelings again. Those feelings were somewhat based on the excitement we felt due to the newness of our relationship.

There was so much to get to know about our partner, so much uncharted territory to explore—what they liked, how they thought, even how they reacted in situations of stress or danger. Our relationships were a daily discovery that unearthed new aspects of this person to whom we were so strongly attracted. Truth is, we can't regain the thrill of that excavation. We've already been there, discovered that. Besides, though it was *a type of love*—one of four we're going to explore in this chapter—it wasn't what real—*by that I mean biblical*—love truly is.

The inability to go back and meet your mate all over again isn't the only trouble with capturing a feeling of love and affection for our spouse. A great deal of the difficulty lies in the fact that we have a warped view of romance. Or maybe it's better to say that we have an *accurate* view of what the *world* calls romance—and it's the world whose views are warped.

Our culture tells us that love:

- is full of tingly feelings of deep longing and intense affection.
- experiences peace and harmony in our interactions.
- unfolds in settings of beauty—at romantic chalets, moonlit beaches, or walks in the park feeling the crisp fall air and viewing gorgeous, colorful leaves on the trees.
- is characterized by our spouses giving us expensive, extravagant, or well-thought-out and meaningful gifts.
- means knowing your partner so well you can finish each other's sentences.
- comes easy.
- is a warm puppy. (Okay, I've never understood this one, but I threw it in anyway!)

The fact that our brains are ever-so-subtly adopting the definition of what culture thinks love means is completely doing us in.

So, what is love—I mean *true* love? There's no better place to look than in the book about the greatest love ever—which demonstrates again and again God's love for us, most of all by sending Jesus to earth to become the sacrifice that took away our sins and offered us a place in eternity with him forever.

Speaking of Jesus . . .

What fabulous lessons we can glean from how he interacted with others while here on earth. No need to turn on a TED Talk. Just flip open a Bible—or tap and scroll your way around its pixilated pages if you use the electronic sort. Throughout the reports in the Gospels (the first four books of the New Testament that give an eyewitness account of Jesus' life), we see Jesus spending his time with all kinds of people.

Jesus didn't limit his social circle to only those who were financially well-off or socially popular. Nor did all his interactions take place with those who aligned themselves with his beliefs. No. He was known for hanging out with shady people, such as tax collectors or those who had no power or influence, such as little children. He threw open his arms to those whom society turned away. Jesus modeled upside-down living and loving. He granted dignity to people and was kind to them because . . . well, they were *people.*

News flash! Your spouse falls into the category of people! In fact, I'm ashamed to admit that often I treat other people much better than I treat my spouse. The stranger at the grocery store standing in line in front of me. The fellow sports mom sitting next to me in the bleachers. Even people who do something that irks me. Like the server who fails to put the jalapeño on my sub when I actually asked for extra. I don't unload on them; I sweetly smile and grant them grace.

All of the directives in Scripture that talk about how we're to treat other people also apply to how we treat our spouse.

There are times when I'm just about ready to open my mouth and let some not-so-nice words fly in my husband's direction that I will stop and give my ready-to-come-unglued self a little reminder. It goes like this:

He's not just my husband. He is also my brother in Christ.

I honestly ask myself, *How would I react if this were one of my Christian guy friends? What if this was a fellow male church member? Would I behave the same way with him?* This line of questioning has saved me from spewing out words I would later regret. So, remember at all times that he is your husband but also your brother—well, you know what I mean! We show love and respect to him as we would to any other person we know.

The Bible is full of information about love. In fact, a quick search on my cell phone's Bible app shows that the word *love* is used 686 times in the Bible. Now, of course the uses of this word are widely varied: the love of God, the love between friends, the love of knowledge and wisdom, the love of money being the root of all kinds of evil.

He's not just my husband. He is also my brother in Christ.

We're going to start by looking at the portions that talk not about *your marriage* but people in general. After all, we've established the fact that your spouse is a person, right?

The book of 1 John in the New Testament is a relatively short book—only five chapters long and a total of 105 verses—yet it mentions love twenty-seven times! Let's pick up this mega lesson on love in 1 John 4:7–12:

> Dear friends, let us love one another, for love comes from God. Everyone who loves has been born of God and knows God. Whoever does not love does not know God, because God is love. This is how God showed his love among us: He sent his one and only Son into the world that we might live through him. This is love: not that we loved God, but that he loved us and sent his Son as an atoning sacrifice for our sins. Dear friends, since God so loved us, we also ought to love one another. No one has ever seen God; but if we love one another, God lives in us and his love is made complete in us.

Before diving into the original language in which this New Testament passage was written—Greek—let's take a step back and consider some obvious discoveries we can make from simply reading the passage slowly and thoroughly.

*Love comes from God—not from our own emotions or from
our desire to respond based on how we are treated.*

*If you are born of God, you are going to love—your loving
others is evidence of your rebirth in Christ.*

*God is love, but it doesn't say that love is God—a popular but
erroneous line of thinking floating around out there that
asserts that if you love (however you choose to define it),
then you are experiencing God.*

*God demonstrated his love toward us by sending Jesus—this
was sacrificial love.*

*Since God loved us, we ought to love one another—this is the
reason we love.*

*If we love one another, God's love lives in us and his love is
made complete.*

Now let's look at one more chunk of 1 John where love is
described:

We love because he first loved us. Whoever claims to love
God yet hates a brother or sister is a liar. For whoever does
not love their brother and sister, whom they have seen,
cannot love God, whom they have not seen. And he has
given us this command: Anyone who loves God must also
love their brother and sister.

1 John 4:19–21

What further deductions can we draw from these four sentences to add to our little discovery session? Plenty!

*We love because God first loved us—it was his plan, and we
are to imitate him.*

If we claim to love God, yet we hate another person, we lie. (Ouch!)

> *How can we claim to love God, whom we have not seen, when*
> *we don't love our brothers and sisters whom we have*
> *seen? (Double ouch!)*
> *God commands that anyone who loves God must also love*
> *their brother and sister. And the last time I checked,*
> *a wife is also considered a sister, and a husband is a*
> *brother too.*

When we not only do a brief read-through of these verses but also internalize them and then live out their principles, it will not only change our *attitudes* toward our husbands but empower us to change our behavior toward them as well.

LEARNING THE LOVE LINGO

Let's drill down yet deeper into the Bible's definition of love. I have found it fascinating to learn over my years of study at college, in church, and on my own that there is more than one word translated as "love" in the Bible. Each word's meaning offers a different impression. Such a concept of varied definitions of love is foreign to us who say (in almost the same breath) that we love our kids and we also love the new pair of shoes we found on clearance at the mall.

In Greek—the native tongue in which the New Testament was written—we find four words for "love": *phileo*, *storge*, *eros*, and *agape*. Here are their basic definitions:

- *Phileo*—used as both a noun and a verb—is an affection, fondness, or appreciation of another that involves giving *to* someone—in part because you've received something *from* them. It's a feeling, a matter of sentiment. Most often this particular word is used to denote

friendship—or brotherly love. The city of Philadelphia?
It's a compound word from *phileo* ("to love") and *adelphos*
("brother").

- *Storge* is an affection that has its basis in nature—such
  as the intrinsic movement of the soul for a close family
  member. The word even has overtones of an obligation
  and is usually used when wanting to communicate the
  love of parents or children. *Of course* we think people
  should love the members of their own family. It's only
  natural, right?

- *Eros* means—I'll bet you can guess by looking at the
  word—erotic love. This doesn't necessarily mean an
  immoral love. It's perfectly appropriate to use the word
  when referring to a husband and wife. This is love based
  on a certain chemistry you feel with another person,
  an overwhelming passion and desire that engulfs your
  very being. Interestingly, even though it's aimed toward
  someone else, it's primarily *self-centered*.

  Eros is a love that results because of the pleasure
  someone brings you. If some component of what caused
  that pleasure ceases to exist, *eros* love fades—or worse—
  converts to intense hatred instead. Why? Because it was
  a selfish rather than a sacrificial love.

- *Agape* is the final and most honorable word for *love* found
  in the Greek language. It is a love that's given not based
  on someone's *deservedness* or performance but *despite*
  their behavior. It chooses to keep delighting in giving,
  even when the other person is unresponsive. It is the type
  of love God has for us—*total and unconditional*.

Now, here's the thing. There are plenty of places where the
friendship type of fondness (*phileo*) is mentioned in the Bible

(John 11:3; 15:19; Titus 3:15, among others). *Phileo* is used to describe the love of Jonathan and David as well as that of Jesus and Peter.

Storge (natural, familial love) is used fairly regularly too, but it has the prefix *a* in front of it, changing the meaning to "unloving." We find examples in Romans 1:31 and 2 Timothy 3:3. *Storge* is also combined with *phileo* in Romans 12:10, translated there as "devoted."

Agape (unconditional love) is used throughout the New Testament more than 320 times! But interestingly enough, this particular word is almost unknown in literature outside of Christian Scripture. Indeed, only a few occurrences of it have ever been discovered elsewhere.

Finally—are you ready for it? The Greek word *eros*—erotic, passionate, self-centered love—is *never* used in the New Testament.

So, when we look at these words for *love* side by side, what can we conclude? I think it looks something like this:

Phileo affection is a growing fondness between two friends that typically develops gradually. It cannot be commanded because it's tied to feelings toward another person, but it *can* develop over time in a relationship. However, given that *phileo* love gives because it receives, it's conditional.

Storge love is natural; it happens intrinsically. And sometimes, we *do* love others—especially family members—out of a sense of obligation because we feel it's the right thing to do.

Eros love certainly occurs in life. In most folks, pretty frequently. No planning required! However, we must realize that, for the most part, it's unsustainable. Furthermore, this intense attraction can often morph, becoming debilitating hatred later on. Haven't we all known people who were once in love and married, but who today voice their intense dislike—even hatred—of the same man or woman who is now their former spouse?

And one more important observation: even though this feelings-driven *eros* love is not always wrong, we are never commanded in the Bible to have this type of love.

Agape is where it's at, people! The supernatural love that originates with God. The kind of love that's a choice. That loves *despite*, not because of. That isn't tied to our emotions as *phileo* is but is rooted in our wills, as we make up our minds to display such sacrificial love to one another. *Agape* is the type of love described in what has come to be known as the "Love Chapter" of the Bible—1 Corinthians 13.

Agape love is an action—not a feeling—that endeavors to display to another human being the unconditional love of God.

If we were to look back at the passages from 1 John that I mentioned earlier and investigate which Greek word for *love* was used, we would see that God is commanding us to display *agape*, unreserved love toward other people. Yes, even people of the spousal sort. This unconditional love shouldn't scare us. If God commands us to display it, *he will enable us to do it*! And remember, this love comes from God himself (1 John 4:7). It isn't something we have to try to muster up from within ourselves. God will give it to us, so we can in turn display it to our spouse.

Long lead-up, I know. But don't miss my point: the sad reality of marital love fading over the years can only truly be understood through the lens of *all* the varied types of love. It looks a little like this:

Couples start off with the passionate, intense attraction (*eros*) that they mistake for true love. Don't get me wrong;

this attraction can be a fine starting point that draws them together and will point them to a true and lasting love—but it isn't the whole chalupa. If the relationship is based solely on this passion, it usually dwindles over time.

The friendship factor (*phileo*) can be a wonderful aspect of a husband-wife relationship and is often missing. If the fondness fades and a friendship never develops—or even more importantly, an *agape* type of love doesn't materialize— many marriages are held together by a flimsy thread of obligatory affection (*storge*) that weakly utters, "Sure, I love my husband. Duh! I *have* to. He's my husband!" I have witnessed a few marriages that lasted for decades but seemed miserable. They stayed together not out of true love, or even due to feelings of fond friendship, but solely out of duty.

Our marriages can (and *ought to*) be characterized by a desire to display *agape* love toward our husband, even though it's so hard at times. Choosing to rely on God for this unconditional love that overlooks an offense, loves despite, forgives always, and forges ahead is our only hope for having both a lasting and a satisfying marriage.

Agape love is the great override button that can help us hang in there and keep showing up.

IF IT IS TO BE, IT IS UP TO ME (WELL, SORTA)

Remember that survey I conducted with a thousand women about marriage? I asked them to travel back in their thoughts to their dating days and give me adjectives and phrases they once thought would characterize their relationships after they walked down the aisle.

Among the words they rattled off: *exciting, romantic, harmonious*; *blissful, adventurous, fulfilling*; *connected, peaceful, magical.* A few even said, "Just like a Hallmark movie!" (Pass the popcorn—and the tissues—please.)

Contrast that with the list of words they used when I asked them to describe what their marriages are really like today. Among those words: *challenging, disappointing, one-sided; combative, routine, disrespectful; lonely, sad, hopeless.*

Now, the words on the second list weren't the only ones listed. A little more than half of the respondents went for more hopeful, healthy words, including *loving, patient, unified* (think friends, partners, teams); *fun, prayerful, strong; peaceful, contented, reliable.* Again, my point here (as throughout this book) is *not* to say that *every* marriage is in crisis. It's to remind us all that *every* marriage can stand to improve. We can learn to show more Christlike love as we grow and mature, both in our relationships with each other and our relationship with God.

Is the unfortunate selection of adjectives I chose to provide in my marriage survey due directly to external circumstances and issues? Sometimes—maybe. You didn't have to read this book to realize that troubles definitely come our way, dire circumstances that rattle our relationship to its very core. But that's not what I'm addressing here.

What I'm thinking of here has to do more with what happens *within* our minds and hearts rather than what happens externally in our life's circumstances. I know this concept well because it has played out in my own life several times. It is this: the trouble with our marriages isn't that we need more excitement in our lives; we need an attitude adjustment.

Yes. An attitude adjustment. Like the on-the-spot lecture I would often give my children back in the day—you know, when they were rolling their eyes at me when asked to do something and they just weren't feeling it, or when they put on a pout because things weren't going their way. I would convincingly instruct them, "Suck it up, buttercup. You need an attitude adjustment." I still say this to myself often, reminding my amnesiac brain that marriage is hard and it's not about me.

A great first step to finding satisfaction and joy in your marriage is to take ownership of your attitude, recognizing that you can choose to have a positive one rather than one that stinks.

Orison Swett Marden, an inspirational author who wrote in the late-nineteenth century, said this—quoting, in part, President Abraham Lincoln: "The sweetest, the most desirable things we know are purchasable only with effort, with right conduct, right thought, right effort. Lincoln said that 'folks are usually about as happy as they make up their minds to be.'"[1]

So, let's make up our minds to be happy. I know, I know, that sounds like a sappy statement of idealism. But it *can* be done. It begins with recognizing an important truth that we wives get oh-so-wrong. You ready?

Your husband is your husband. He is not God.

Oh boy, do we get this wrong! We place expectations on our husband that only God can fulfill.

Only God can meet our needs.
Only God can make us truly joyful.
Only God has endless patience, all the answers, and an
    unconditional love for us that never wanes or runs out.
Only. God.

God is God. Your husband is not. Stop putting so much pressure on the poor man, expecting him to meet your every need—even if he does a rather stellar job at trying. Acting as God is exhausting for your husband and only sets you up for failure when you expect him to fulfill this role. He can't. Ever. Not even for a moment.

My friend Lysa once said something astonishing to me during a time in my marriage when I was looking to Todd for my joy in life rather than looking to God. I hope it shakes you up like it did me. She rightly asserted, "Even the very best husband makes a very poor God."

Yes, and amen.

When we even ever so subtly assume that it is our husband's role to meet all our needs, not only will we be disappointed, but we will have the entirely wrong view of marriage.

So let's remember our spouse's role. And God's. You game? And then repeat after me: *My husband is my husband. He is not my God.* Good work!

When we have our heads screwed on right—as my mama used to say—then we can make up our minds to be joyful, even during the frustrating times in our marriage.

Say what?

Yes. We can choose to delight even in the turbulent times, the annoying times, the times we want to hit the delete button on

My husband is my husband. He is not my God.

our relationship and start creating an online dating profile, but we press on and persevere anyway. Why? By savoring this truth . . .

Your marriage can be the tool God uses to renovate your heart, making you more like Jesus.

Choose to view your marriage as an exhilarating excursion because through it your sandpaper spouse is helping grow your relationship with God, helping make you look more like his Son to the watching world. So stop trying to change your husband. Change your attitude instead.

Now, I know that for some wives, the problem stems less from expecting your husband to be like God—meeting your needs—and has more to do with your belief that he is acting so *unlike* God that you sometimes think of him as the enemy. What then?

Then—we still show love.

To his disciples and the crowd that had gathered around him, Jesus said, "Whoever wants to be my disciple must deny themselves and take up their cross and follow me. For whoever wants to save their life will lose it, but whoever loses their life *for me and for the gospel will save it*" (Mark 8:34–35, emphasis mine).

This is a true test of our faith—losing our lives for Christ and the gospel.

It's easy to love those who are lovable. But Christ calls us to do the seemingly impossible sometimes—to love someone you deem an enemy. Perhaps you view your husband as an adversary due to whatever constant area of struggle you have—the issue that threatens to drive a wedge between the two of you because you can't seem to deal with it directly and properly and then forgive and move on. The thin edge of the wedge works its way in repeatedly as you revisit—but never resolve—the issue.

It reminds me of my email app. When an email comes up that I don't feel like dealing with, I tap the snooze button. The message will then be sent to me another day. But when it reappears, what if I *still* don't want to monkey around with it? I keep snoozing, and it keeps rearing its bothersome head because I never stop and actually deal with the crazy thing!

When you adopt the view that your husband is your enemy, it does not grant you the right to behave wrongly toward him. Jesus calls us to countercultural behavior. He even calls us to love our enemies. Period.

So, whether you think your man is so splendid that he's right up there next to God, or he is someone you struggle to display love to because of his indifferent or unbecoming behavior, let's seek an attitude adjustment by keeping in mind the following points.

Love is a choice to make. Not trying to beat you over the head with this one, but it is the foundation for all the others. *Agape* love is not a feeling; it is a choice. Choose it daily. Choose it often. Choose it even when you seriously don't care to. Keep showing up and keep choosing love.

Love is a chance to serve. Jesus calls us to a lay-down-your-life sort of service. We are to put others' interests ahead of our own. The apostle Paul urges this: "Do nothing out of selfish ambition or vain conceit. Rather, in humility value others above yourselves, not looking to your own interests but each of you to the interests of the others" (Philippians 2:3–4). Be on the lookout for ways to serve your husband, to put his interests and desires before your own. Remember that when you serve, you aren't just serving your hubby; you are also serving Jesus.

He is not your God, but he bears God's image. When God made humans in his likeness, the result was that all human beings carry what is known theologically as the *imago Dei*—the quality that sets humans apart from other creatures. When we look into the eyes of another human being—especially our husband—may we be aware that we are dealing with someone made in the very image of our Creator. Treat him accordingly.

Don't follow your heart; follow God's Word. Oh, how I cringe every time I spy a whimsical coffee mug or exquisite watercolor painting that urges "Follow Your Heart." Although I know this catchy phrase wasn't meant to be anything more than an encouragement to think confidently, actually following your heart at times can get you in a tornado of trouble. God's Word goes so far as to say that the human heart cannot be trusted: "The heart is deceitful above all things and beyond cure. Who can understand it?" (Jeremiah 17:9). So, keep your nose in God's Word—dragging your mind along for the ride. Read it. Study it. Memorize it. God's Word is to be followed, even during those times when it conflicts with your feelings. Trust the truths of Scripture. You can't go wrong by doing the right—and righteous—things outlined on the pages of the Bible.

Don't think marriage is about finding the right person. It's about striving to be the right person. Many marital hopes have been dashed because a bride set out to find the right person to marry. We get this so backward! It's not about finding that perfect match for you. Even if you found someone you thought was perfect, you can't make them stay that way. You cannot control another person's behavior, no matter how strongly you believe you can. The only thing you can control is yourself—your attitudes, actions, and reactions. Spend your energy on attempting to be the right person—the one who follows God and his ways. Insisting that your husband line up with your expectations of what a Prince Charming should be only brings about disappointment. This leads us to our next goal . . .

Make it a contest. Yes. A contest. But not one your husband knows you are a participant in. The contest's one rule is found in Romans 12:10 (CSB): "Love one another deeply as brothers and sisters. Outdo one another in showing honor." Don't keep score of how many kind gestures your husband makes toward you. Just endeavor to keep the honor, love, and kind deeds flowing in his general direction. Television news personality Diane Sawyer made this accurate observation: "A good marriage is a contest of generosity."[2] So true! But remember, we aren't granted access to heaven by the good deeds shown to our husbands—or to anyone for that matter. Salvation is based on Jesus' sacrifice on our behalf, not on any do-gooding we may do. God doesn't need our good deeds, but our husbands often do.

Think of the first day . . . and the last day. One of the best pieces of marital advice I ever heard was from my friend Becky Thompson, author of *Love Unending: Rediscovering Your*

Marriage in the Midst of Motherhood.[3] She was recently my guest on a Facebook Live session I held for my followers on the topic of marriage. During our interview, she gave me—and my online friends—some valuable advice. Her father had first shared it with her, and she called it a forty-year-old secret. She also said it helped save her marriage. This key to a successful marriage? It could fit in a Tweet. He said, "Becky, every day I wake up, I tell myself that it's the first day I am married to your mom."

What would it look like to follow this advice? Becky describes it this way: "I suppose on my wedding day, I didn't bark at my husband, 'Get up and come help me!' I was kind. I didn't avoid touching him because I was 'touched out' by my little kids. I was his bride! I didn't tune him out when he spoke because I just couldn't handle one more story and was desperate for some mental space. I tuned in. Could someone really live like that every day?" Becky says that for her, this was a crucial turning point. She began to make it her goal, each time she shut off the alarm and crawled out of the covers, to think back to that very first morning and treat her husband like she did when he was her new groom many years ago.

Not only is it helpful to rewind our minds back in time, but our perspectives can be shifted by also thinking ahead. I like to ask myself questions that can empower me to make right choices by starting them with another tweetable sentiment: "Someday, looking back from the grave . . ." It helps me make decisions more easily. Like, "Someday, looking back from the grave, will I be more thankful that I attended yet another product party at a friend's home—my fourth such get-together that year—or that I brought my aging father a pizza and we split it while watching a Detroit Tigers game on TV?" See? Easy answer!

When it comes to how we treat our husbands, vigilantly thinking through our words and actions by asking ourselves a question that begins with "someday, looking back from the grave ..." can help us to choose our behavior wisely. *Make choices today that won't cause regret tomorrow.* Someday, near the end of life, will you be thankful you made the choices you did when it comes to how you interact with your husband? It can save you a big bundle of anguish and regret, wishing so desperately that you could then have do-overs.

You can't. But you *can* begin now to prevent such episodes of remorse from happening in the first place.

This starts when we determine to stop defining love and romance the way our culture does. When we choose to display no-strings-attached love to our partners even when they don't deserve it. To see shared work around the house as an opportunity to forge the friendship part of our relationship. To laugh at ourselves and at each other—often and heartily. To share a common goal of living out the gospel before the eyes of all who are watching—especially our kids.

Pick love when you'd rather pick a fight.

Most of all, when we adopt a mind-set that decides that we will *choose love* and *display joy*, not because of our spouse's behavior but despite it.

Yes, *despite* it.

Pick love when you'd rather pick a fight.

Just keep showing up.

SIX

FINDING MAGIC IN THE MUNDANE

*Marriage is not just spiritual communion
and passionate embraces; marriage is also
three meals a day, sharing the workload,
and remembering to carry out the trash.*

DR. JOYCE BROTHERS

*Satisfy us in the morning with your unfailing love,
that we may sing for joy and be glad all our days.*

PSALM 90:14

For all of my decades of life (and no, I won't say how many that is), I've lived in the Great Lakes State—the Mitten State that is the land of Michigan. It's known as #PureMichigan to those of us who like to help market our region, inviting others to "come and experience our four beautiful seasons and our five fabulous freshwater lakes." We Michiganders even carry our beloved state's map with us wherever we go—in the form of our hand. This way we can easily point to where our city, town, or village is on our *handy* (get it?) map. (My little town is smack-dab in the middle of the mitten, in case you were wondering.)

I like to think of our state as America's high five.

A few years ago, a local campaign began in nearby Lansing, Michigan's capital city, where I was born. It was called "Be a Tourist in Your Own Town." This one-day event promoted more than seventy-five local attractions and offered transportation between them by selling bus tickets for just fifty cents.

The featured stops spanned a wide gamut. There were behind-the-scenes tours where you could discover how coffee beans are roasted, the nightly newscast is produced, or a local brand of soda pop is crafted. You could browse the Michigan Women's Historical Center, the R. E. Olds (Oldsmobile's founder) transportation museum, or the local school for the blind where Stevie Wonder was once a student. Families could paint, throw pottery, roller-skate, or try their hand at sidewalk chalk art. So many activities that you couldn't possibly do them all in that one day.

I was flabbergasted by this clever endeavor. Not only because it was well organized, educational, and loads of fun, but because I would venture to guess that—even though I've lived in mid-Michigan for all but one of my years—I had never even heard of more than half of these local attractions, landmarks, and buildings.

Sometimes we don't notice the delights right in front of us because we're too busy just going about our regular—and often mundane—routine.

The familiar and repetitive nature of life can nestle us into a predictable rhythm of humdrum. Oh, we keep going and functioning, swiping right each morning to reveal a new page on our digital calendars. But nothing else is new or exciting, right? In fact, it's rather lackluster. Where is the spark? The anticipation of discovery? Why, we'd settle for even a tiny bit of passion.

What is a bored-out-of-her-gourd gal to do?

It's time we reframed romance.

RETHINKING ROMANCE

I've spent a lot of time over the past twenty-plus years in ministry either speaking on a stage somewhere in the nation—wearing cute-but-still-comfy shoes—or writing from the desk in my tiny aqua office at home, sipping coffee and wearing fuzzy socks. Both places have afforded me the opportunity and pleasure of interacting with all kinds of women.

Many women approach me at my book table to ask questions or email them to me through my website. Of course, I can't answer them all adequately—due to lack of time, lack of expertise, or both! I make sure people know I am not a trained counselor or a relationship expert. I'm just someone who loves to teach from Scripture and then to share what God has taught me, in case it might also help someone else.

The questions tossed my way are on a wide variety of topics. Some are rather trivial, such as an Instagram follower sending me a message, inquiring, "Hey. Where did you get that aqua mixing bowl I see in the background of your latest picture?" (I'll bet you can now guess what my favorite color is!)

Perhaps the question I'm asked most frequently when a woman pulls me aside privately at an event is, "What can I do? My husband and I don't seem to be in love anymore." Often it's said with desperation in their words and tears welling up in their eyes.

When I probe further by asking some clarifying questions, I find that for many of them, there is no major issue. No financial crisis. No infidelity. No physical or emotional abuse. Just this overall sense of "ho-hum" boredom and an excruciatingly noticeable lack of love.

Oh, they still manage to function. The trash gets taken out. The bills are paid. The gas tanks are filled. The kids get shuffled to their sports and activities. But just getting all the household tasks completed and the appointments kept does not equal a marriage.

That's not a marriage—*that's an arrangement.*

Arrangements do not fulfill us emotionally. Their lackluster existence signals to us that something is dreadfully wrong.

Each marital "arrangement" is unique. And so there are no slap-on-a-Bible-verse, universal answers. However, a few common threads appear as I listen to women bemoan their loveless marriages. They usually have to do with one of these two issues: (1) a skewed view of romance or (2) a misunderstanding of how they and their spouses show love.

When one (or both!) of these is present in a marriage, it can lead to an overall sense that they are trapped in a loveless relationship. Let's tackle these two issues and see if working through them might help dissolve an "arrangement" and help a healthy, loving marriage emerge in its place.

SKEWED VIEW OR REAL ROMANCE?

I'm so glad that my husband and I got engaged before the era of Facebook and Instagram. There's so much pressure these days when it comes to pulling out all the stops while popping the question. Just do a quick search online for the most romantic proposals. Or the most creative proposals. Or even those where the bride is surprised by a flash mob, as hundreds of people break out singing in harmony while also performing elaborate choreography. Oh, and it's all conveniently captured from four different camera angles and spliced together in a film that racks up millions of views and goes viral!

Now, I don't knock a modern-day, pull-out-all-the-stops creative proposal. They are undoubtedly entertaining to watch.

And they certainly show a guy's willingness to put time into something that will speak love to his lady. But sometimes all of this "high bar" setting can start to set up a false notion of what romance is. So can elaborate weddings. And over-the-top honeymoons.

You see, sometimes we spend a massive amount of time staging and planning our weddings and very little time sincerely trying to discern what real romance and true love actually are.

True love isn't a man who will race through the rain down a crowded city street to passionately embrace his wife, beseeching her to return after a lovers' quarrel.

Real romance doesn't come with a hefty price tag or show its affections by emptying a bank account—or worse, by going deep into debt—in order to prove its intense longings for another.

True love isn't flashy, wanting others outside of your marriage to cheer and applaud your showy efforts.

Authentic love isn't proven by dramatic gestures, expensive rings, or attention-getting tactics. Not at all.

So, what is it then?

True love is the steadfast presence of your lover, the willingness to stick it out when things get rocky. It demonstrates love when no one else is looking. True love is wholly committed, costing the giver time and effort. It gives with no expectation of recognition or return.

True love seeks to lighten the other's load. It attempts to understand the other's feelings, to soothe the unsettled soul of its love.

Real romance takes out the trash without being reminded, changes the baby's diaper when Mama is plain tuckered out, or swings by the husband's office just to drop off his favorite snack for his afternoon break.

True love models Christ by laying down its rights—and

seeking to do no wrong. It places the other's wishes above its own.

True love is not a public fist pump. It loves in the secret places of the heart and then shows it in quiet ways, right there in the microscopic, mundane minutes of life.

I've been a student in the classroom of real love for decades now. Oh, how my views of what romance *really* is have changed!

I used to want Todd to buy me flowers. Not just any flowers, mind you; I wanted the ones sold in a fancy floral shop. They come in an elegant white box, fastened shut with a gold seal and tied up tight with a big, shimmery bow. Years ago, if Todd would have brought me a simple bouquet from the grocery store— decorated not with a seal and a bow but only with a bright orange clearance sticker—I would have concluded that he didn't really love me.

Fast-forward a decade or two. Now we had a mortgage. And three kiddos to feed. We were living on one quite-below-average income. If my dear hubby would have purchased the fancy-pants flowers and brought them home to me during that season of life, he wouldn't have been met with a thank-you kiss but with a wife coming ever-so-slightly (but rightly!) unglued, proclaiming, "What? Are you crazy? We can't afford to drop that kind of money on flowers that will die in a few days!"

Over the years, I've learned to appreciate when he comes home with a neon-stickered, supermarket spray of on-clearance roses. His way of impressing me now lies in getting those babies at the lowest price possible. His current record is a dozen peach roses—the color we had in our wedding—for only two bucks! Better yet, my heart flutters when he's out weeding and stops to pick a rogue daisy that is growing wild between the sage and rosemary in my herb garden. He knocks on the back-deck door, and when I open it, he presents it, saying sheepishly, "I like you."

Likewise, my heart melts, not when he drops a bunch of money on some jewelry, but when he drops by the airport on his way home from work on a bitterly cold Michigan winter afternoon to locate my car in the parking lot and scrape off two days' worth of accumulated snow because he knows my flight returns a few hours later.

The whole romanticized notion today of a "soul mate" has ruined many a marriage. The image and behavior associated with it just can't be sustained. I do better thinking of my husband, not as my soul mate, but as my *sole* mate—meaning he is the one and only for me.

Wives. Listen to me. Once we've walked down the aisle, we have no more need to look around at other men who might make a better husband. This is so dangerous! I have known four women—I don't mean

> *No man was ever shot while unloading the dishwasher.*
>
> *Anonymous*

I've read about them online; I mean I know them in real life—who connected through social media with either a former boyfriend or a brand-new man and then decided to divorce their husbands and leave their children to ride off happily into the sunset. And no, none of those resulting relationships made the women any happier. In fact, all but one of these relationships also failed!

We are duped into believing that a new man (or a nostalgic and familiar man from our past) will make us happy. But counselors will tell you that their offices are filled with people who left their first marriage for a reason other than biblical grounds and then wound up just as miserable as they were with their former spouse. Many even more so.

Throughout the seasons of marriage, romance itself "seasons"—it grows up and matures. We can learn to notice the quiet gestures of love when we stop looking for the flashy and obvious long enough to notice the unassuming and inconspic-uous instead.

Do you know how I now interpret Todd's love for me? It's not measured in costly gifts or romantic weekend getaways. I'm not shown love by any eloquent speeches of all the qualities he adores in me. Nope. My guy is a man of very few words.

Over the years, I've come to recognize his love for me in other ways. When I spy the kitchen counter emptied of the heap of dirty dishes I just couldn't seem to get to that day. By his willingness when the kids were small to serve on clean-up duty after one of them got sick in the wee hours of the night. By the full tank of gas in our vehicle I rarely have to think about—let alone pump.

My guy doesn't show love to me the way I used to think a man should. Nor does he express love the way I do. If I'd never learned how to recognize love in his specific way of conveying it, I would have continued to believe the lie that he really didn't love me.

He did.

The problem was we just weren't talking in the same tongue.

SHOW ME THE LOVE

When my new groom and I were in that first two-year span of awfulness, he tried to show me love. Really, he tried. And so did I.

He grew up with a very quiet, unassuming father who worked hard both in his career as a car salesman and at home around the house and yard. He was steady. A rock. Kind to everyone he met. He was a quiet, behind-the-scenes sort of servant rather than a "Here I am—let's talk!" sort of guy. Todd is nearly the same in demeanor. Neither of them needed much to keep them happy, and they certainly didn't need material items.

When we were first married, I often felt that Todd didn't love me. And so I told him so! He just couldn't understand what in the world I was talking about. After all, he would clean our entire apartment on his day off when I was at my job as a substitute teacher and coach. He'd even have a homemade pizza ready to pop in the oven for our dinner that night.

He'd take the soiled clothes, sheets, and towels down to the laundry room in our apartment house basement, washing them all and then drying them and putting them all away. He always washed any dishes he saw collecting in the sink. To him, lightening my load around the house and helping to get errands done were how one showed love. The trouble is, I couldn't have cared less about these things! I really don't mind housework.

I thought love would be evidenced by him stopping in the middle of his day to phone me and tell me what a fabulous wife he thought I was—citing specific examples of my wonderfulness, of course. Or I wanted him to leave me a handwritten love note on my pillow with my favorite candy bar—a York Peppermint Pattie. Or buy me a rose and drop it off at the school—you know, so all my coworkers could also witness his deep devotion to me! After all, these were the things I did for him—verbally praising him or gifting him with a little tangible token of my affection. But these gestures toward him fell flat. They didn't communicate love to him.

We found out what our problem was when we discovered the concept of love languages made famous by Dr. Gary Chapman.[1] (And I'm talking *fay-mous*. His book *The Five Love Languages* has sold more than eleven million copies and has been translated into fifty languages!)

Over his many years of counseling couples, Dr. Chapman started to see a pattern emerge. The wife in a couple would verbalize how she did not feel loved. However, her husband would cite all the ways he had shown love to her. Then it was the husband's turn. He would also assert that he wasn't feeling the love from his wife. But then she would chime in listing all the ways she had displayed love. As Dr. Chapman listened, he discovered a fascinating dynamic that led to his theory of people possessing five different love languages.

The basic concept is that we all have a primary language for giving and receiving love. Where the confusion comes in is when both spouses don't speak the same language.

The five languages Dr. Chapman discovered are:

- words of affirmation
- acts of service
- receiving gifts
- quality time
- physical touch

To the person whose language is *words of affirmation*, actions do *not* speak louder than words. They want the words. ALL. THE. WORDS. Talk to them already! Jot them a note. Send them a text. Anything that is bursting with words of what you value and appreciate about them. This fills their heart to the brim.

The folks who have the love language of *acts of service* interpret love as someone doing something to help them "get life done." They feel love when you walk the dog, take out the trash, run the errand, or clear the dirty dishes off the table so they don't have to. Such actions convey love to them.

Those who love *receiving gifts* want someone who will think of them while out and about during the day and pick them up a small remembrance. It doesn't have to be expensive. Any little token speaks libraries of love to them. Don't misconstrue this as materialism. It isn't the "gifted" item that's important; it's the thoughtfulness and effort behind it.

Next is *quality time*. If this is your love language, you want your spouse to be not only nearby in physical proximity but fully engaged relationally. You equate love with undivided attention. It's important to you that your spouse be all there—*really* there—without cell phones beeping and buzzing, competing with you for their attention. *Love* to you is a four-letter word spelled T-I-M-E.

And finally, *physical touch* people? Yep, they are those touchy-feely types—in a good way! They crave simple gestures like snuggling up to watch a show, holding hands on a walk, receiving a heartfelt hug hello or good-bye, even being gently touched on the shoulder. This doesn't have to include "horizontal friendship" (wink, wink), though sometimes it does. These folks show love with their "reach out and touch someone" ways.

Well, you can easily see what was happening in my marriage. My primary love language is words of affirmation, followed closely by receiving gifts. So, talk to me, baby—or give me a little something—and I will feel the love all day long.

However, when it comes to showing affection, Todd rolls a whole different way. His love language is acts of service. Lots of service. In both family life and outside of our four walls, he can be counted on to pitch in and help, to lessen another person's workload, to quietly labor as a way to demonstrate love.

Since we spoke different love languages, the result was much like putting two people together from different countries who do not speak each other's native tongue. They can flap their gums all they want to, but they will have no idea what the other one is saying. They are incapable of comprehending what the other person is trying desperately to communicate.

Most of Todd's acts of service went unnoticed by me. I was yearning for him to talk to me, mentioning specific things he appreciated about me. Or I was looking for clever love notes left around the house. Or expecting thoughtful gifts to appear. And what would really send me over the top would be if he gave me a gift while *also* verbally telling me how much I meant to him. In my book, that was the epitome of love.

This mismatched dynamic works the other way as well. Here's how: I assumed I was clearly demonstrating love toward my husband by strategically placing little notes in his briefcase or on his side of the bed. I bought him inexpensive gifts. And I always had a sentimental speech on standby, ready in a heartbeat to verbally tell him how fabulous I thought he was.

However, Todd would have much rather had me assist him with some task. At that time, he was a youth pastor in charge of three different youth groups at church, as well as being the one responsible for teaching the high school Bible class on Sunday mornings. If I would have put my energies into setting up the meetings, preparing for the crazy games we played, or taking care of ordering the pizza and purchasing paper goods and soda pop, it would have shouted love to him. He could have done without the tiny trinkets and talk.

I can't stress enough how imperative I think it is for you and your spouse to understand these love languages. You can learn more about them—and take a free assessment test that will reveal which languages you possess—by visiting www.5lovelanguages.com. It can really help strengthen your relationship and clear up those feelings of "he doesn't love me!" It may be that you were looking for love in a bouquet of flowers, and it was right there all along in an empty trash can or a loaded dishwasher!

HOW BORING CAN BE BEAUTIFUL

One afternoon, I took a break from sorting through the ever-growing pile of papers on my desk, to warm up my coffee and hop on Twitter for a few moments to catch up on what was going on in the world. As I was tapping and scrolling, I happened upon a Tweet that read, "All I want is a love like Chip and Joanna's." The writer of the hopeful Tweet was referring to Chip and Joanna Gaines, stars of the hit HGTV show *Fixer Upper*. In case you've been living under a rock and don't recognize their names, this Texas couple hosted a widely watched home improvement show in which they took homes in desperate need of remodeling and did a major overhaul on them, turning them into their clients' dream homes.

The show drew viewers by the millions. However, they weren't *all* tuning in to see the farm sinks and shiplap—or the fancy new counters the couple installed. I think just as many were flipping on their TVs to see the Gaineses' interaction as husband and wife.

The day I saw the Tweet, I did a little detective work, searching some keywords in the search bar on Twitter. I discovered dozens, if not hundreds, of people saying the same thing. All they wanted in life was a love like Chip and Joanna's.

Here is what I love about people longing for their relationship to emulate that of the Gaineses. Most likely it doesn't have to do with anything fancy, extravagant, or expensive. I don't think people are jealous of their marriage. I think instead they honestly want to know how to build one like it themselves.

Usually the show featured the Gaineses' banter as husband and wife, as they often teased each other. They'd even poke fun at their personality differences. They were polite as they interacted, even though sometimes you could tell that they each got on each other's nerves. Chip's antics often embarrassed Joanna, especially when they were antique hunting for items to go in their clients' homes. And he got frustrated at her desire to sometimes switch things up mid-project. However, their interactions over these issues were *healthy*. They were pleasant with each other, but also direct.

And they were so endearing! He called her Jo-Jo. She always told him, "Thanks, Chip" when leaving the premises after checking up on his work. Their love was simple and often silly. But you could sense they genuinely enjoyed each other's company, and they seemed to have a spark in their eyes as they looked at each other. Of course, you could argue that this was all done for the camera, but it just didn't seem that they were putting on a show (pun totally intended).

Here's the thing: any couple can cultivate a love like Chip and Joanna seem to have. You know why? The Gaineses have made it abundantly clear in articles and interviews that their marriage is based on the faith in Jesus that they both share. The radical love of Jesus engulfs them, empowering them to fiercely love each other. And all of us are capable of going to Jesus for the same strength and resolve to love our spouse as the Bible commands—with a smidgeon of simple, silly love tossed in for good measure, of course.

When we don't have a skewed or unrealistic view of romance but understand and apply what the Bible teaches about love, and when we start speaking to our spouse in their native love language, we can unearth the magic in the midst of the mundane—those daily days of marriage. Here are some ways to do that.

Go Back in Time

While we cannot recreate the feelings of excitement and newness we felt when we were first getting to know our spouse, we can think of the character qualities that most attracted us to them.

Write down two or three characteristics you most appreciated about your spouse. How have you seen those characteristics play out over the years you've been married? Let your husband know how much you've appreciated seeing those qualities in him over the years. But do it in keeping with his love language.

You can write him a note (words of affirmation), tell it to him on a long walk (quality time), or perform one of the chores he normally does and then tell him you did it because you wanted to let him know how much you admire the quality you identified (acts of service). You can buy him his favorite sweet treat and leave it on his pillow with a note attached, telling him what you admire in him (receiving gifts). Or you can pull him in close as you cuddle on the couch and whisper what you appreciate about him into his ear (physical touch).

Let Love Mature

Over the seasons of marriage, love grows up. Try not to expect the typical expressions depicted in Hollywood to be the norm in your marriage. Keeping in mind your husband's love language, look for signs in places other than chocolates, flowers, and jewelry. Maybe it's your husband cleaning out the trash from your car because he performs acts of service to show his love. Or it may be your man just wanting to spend time sitting next to you watching television because, to him, that's a gesture of love: quality time equals love. Also, sometimes the best method of operating is not to expect anything at all. When we don't have any expectations, we can't be disappointed, right? Then even small gestures tickle us pink because we weren't anticipating anything at all.

Display Tangible Signs of Your Union

This is one thing I've done over the past decades that I didn't even know was helping until someone pointed it out to me. Todd and I have many objects around our house that give a nod to our marriage. We have one of our wedding portraits displayed on the wall in our living room, just underneath a rustic wooden sign hand-lettered with 1 Corinthians 13:4: "Love is patient. Love is kind." We have some hand-carved wooden bowls on our dining room table. The larger one has Todd's full name carved around the edge of the inside of the bowl. A smaller one nests perfectly inside of it with my full name carved in the same way. We also have a hand-painted crock that has our names and wedding date on it, given to us by his parents.

These items catch my eye often during the day, reminding me of our love. A friend who stopped over pointed out to me how clever it was that I had all these items strategically worked into our decor to remember the importance of our union. Because most of them were gifts, the thought never crossed my mind that I was doing it on purpose. I was simply displaying items we'd been given.

But you know, I think there is something to what she said. Sometimes, when I'm trying to cool off in the aftermath of a heated discussion, one of these items will catch my eye, reminding me of our vows; reminding me that marriage is hard and it's not about me; and reminding me that my marriage was designed to display the gospel to a watching world and to make me godlier, not giddier. Having such displays of your union around the house can help snap your soul to attention, get your thinking back on track, and prompt you to work toward reconciliation during one of the distressing times in your relationship.

Get to Know Each Other All Over Again

Bust up the boredom by getting to know your spouse all over again, asking them to share their thoughts on anything from their favorite toy growing up to the one thing they've always wanted to try but were afraid to. To make it a snap to do this, check out the section (page 142) at the end of this chapter that lists some fun getting-to-know-you-again date night questions. Head out for a meal, go to a local park, or sit at a sidewalk table at a bistro. Take this book with you and take turns answering the questions listed. I'll bet you discover some things you never knew about each other.

Put in the Hours

In our culture, we don't always like to work hard. We much prefer that things come easy. Oh, we want results—we just don't always want to put the sweat and effort into achieving those results. Or we want shortcuts. I think of all those meal-prep delivery services out there that allow you to throw together a semi-home-cooked meal without having to think through a shopping list, trek off to the store, and then return home to turn your staple items into a meal. Just open a box, throw the already sliced and diced items into a pan, heat it up—and voilà, a home-made feast is served!

We do the same with our marriages. We want a love like Chip and Joanna's—or like _____ and _____'s (fill in the blank with a Christian couple you know), but we don't want to put in any hard work. I know in my own experience, during the times my marriage was *hardly working*, usually it was because I didn't want to work hard. It's hard work to lower your expectations. It's hard work to attempt to communicate clearly, yet kindly. It is for sure hard work to forgive when you feel offended or wronged.

Marriage isn't easy-breezy, but it can be a labor of love when we maintain the mind-set that we are loving and forgiving because Christ calls us to *and* because we want a love that is strong and true.

Have Fun and Be Funny

"A cheerful heart is good medicine, but a crushed spirit dries up the bones" (Proverbs 17:22). Sometimes the prescription our ailing marriage needs is a little bit of laughter and fun.

Speaker and artist Jackie Hill Perry wrote on Twitter recently, "Love should feel like a fun forever."[2] (Amen, sister! One more time for the folks in the back!) Marriage should be fun—and funny. Whatever *you as a couple* determine to be fun.

I know couples who enjoy going to car races. Or the theatre. Some are crazy football fans who never miss a game. Dear friends of ours who live out in the country drive into our little burg each night to walk two miles around town, which they think is fun. Others love to rough it in the wilderness while camping. (Me . . . not so much. Todd and I have gone camping before, but my idea of roughing it is more like when the hotel doesn't have complimentary coffee in the lobby!) Pick yourselves a fun marital hobby that both of you equally enjoy—and look forward to doing—and then do it as often as you can.

That addresses the fun. Now let's talk funny.

Laughter can be worked into marriage in a myriad of ways. Share private jokes. Say goofy things to each other. Our standing cheesy wisecrack for years has been this: one of us calls or texts the other randomly during the day asking, "Hey. Are you tired? You must be, because you've been running through my mind all day!" (Corny as a tortilla chip, I know!)

Lately I've introduced my better half to a fun GIF app (GIF stands for graphic interchange format) that has an almost endless supply of these seconds-long moving graphics that combine a snippet of a video with written text. Now, often we simply talk back and forth in our text message thread by using GIFs, being sure not to get racy, of course. (*Note to Self:* Make sure it's your *husband* you're texting, not the pastor whose name also starts with the letters "T-O." Gulp!)

Okay, so here's a homework assignment for you: become a studious pupil with your husband as the topic of study. Observe him. Find out his love language. (Maybe he won't take the online test, but you can go through the questions, keeping him in mind, and probably figure it out yourself!) Pray to God, asking him to help you accurately display love toward your husband in a way he can easily grasp. You want him to get the message loud and clear—you are crazy in love with him, even though at times he does drive you crazy. (You can just leave that second part off!)

Put in an all-out effort to get to know your husband even better than Google Ads already knows him. (All right—maybe that's a bit of a stretch.)

Keep looking for the magic in the midst of the mundane.

Embrace the combo plate of uniqueness you create as husband and wife. Look for the camouflaged signs of love that exist in your marriage. They are there—you just have to hunt for them sometimes.

There can be elation in the wedded excursion you and your mate are on. Your ordinary marriage can exhibit to others the unending, unswerving, faithful love of God.

Continue to let Christ work in your heart. Then someday you'll encounter someone who says about you and your husband, when they witness God's love flowing between you two, "All I want is a love like _____ and _____'s."

Yes, fill in your names. Believe that it will come true. Let God do the work only he can do.

In the meantime, just keep looking for the magic in the midst of the mundane.

GETTING-TO-KNOW-YOU-AGAIN DATE NIGHT
QUESTIONS

Grab your spouse and head out for a date. It can be having dinner at a fancy restaurant or simply going to a local park to enjoy an ice cream cone or a picnic. Take turns asking the questions below in an effort to get to know your spouse again. You may discover some things you never knew. Happy dating!

1. What television show was your favorite as a child growing up and why? Do you remember a specific episode you loved most?

2. What was your favorite subject in high school? Do you remember anything about your teacher?

3. If you could travel to a state or country that you haven't been to before, where would it be?

4. If you could have any job in the world, which one would you choose?

5. Name your favorite of the following: Color. Soft drink. Candy bar. Main dish food. Fruit. Vegetable. Dessert. Musical group or artist. Book you've read. Movie you've seen. Commercial you remember. Sport or hobby.

6. Did you have a pet growing up? If so, what kind was it and what was his or her name?

7. If you could meet one person in the world—present or past—who would it be and why? What would you ask him or her?

8. Describe the perfect Saturday. What would you do? Where would you go? Or would it be spent doing nothing?
9. When was the first time you ever remember seeing me? Do you remember what your first impression of me was?
10. Do you remember anything about our first date? If so, what?
11. What is the one quality about me that you loved most when we were first getting to know each other?
12. Where would you like to see us ten years from now? What would we be doing and where would we be living?

SEVEN

THE MISSION OF YOUR MARRIAGE

*Forgive me for being so ordinary while
claiming to know so extraordinary a God.*

JIM ELLIOT

*Glorify the LORD with me; let us
exalt his name together.*

PSALM 34:3

Every year without fail, somebody I know has a senior graduating from high school. Here in my hometown, such graduations are no small happenings. We throw graduation open houses like nobody's business. We held such shindigs for each of our three children, as well as another one for our "sorta son" Jacob, who lived with us for a while. We erected big tents, draped "Congratulations" banners in the school colors, displayed oodles of picture boards chronicling the growing-up days of the graduate, and, most importantly, bought, made, and served lots of food. Usually pulled pork or our locally famous sloppy joes with the secret ingredient folks use around here—a can of condensed vegetable soup. (Well, I guess it isn't a secret anymore!)

Guests at these bashes bring scads of cards filled with cash and checks. When receiving such generous gifts, our kids were required to do two things. They had to send a handwritten thank-you note to each person who gave them money, and they must visit with each guest at the open house, prepared to answer the question that would be asked of them dozens of times that day: "What do you plan to do with your life?"

This question isn't just asked of recent grads. Even as small children, we were probably asked more than a time or two what we wanted to do when we grew up. Dreaming about your future was fun, whether you wanted to be an astronaut or an artist, a surgeon or a stay-at-home mom. But now that we're adults, are our dreaming days over? No, not at all.

Don't quit your daydream. Grab your spouse's hand, and together you can find a new one.

The mission of marriage is to make the relationship of Christ and the church come alive. This is primary and of utmost importance. However, each marriage is a blend of two distinct individuals. This duo comes together to form a team uniquely qualified to carry out a mission locally, right in their own backyard.

If you've never thought of your marriage in this way, you're missing an entire fulfilling facet of the marriage relationship. You and your spouse have a combined set of strengths, passions, gifts, and opportunities that—when harnessed properly and prayerfully—can be used by God to spread the gospel and meet the needs of others around you. You can have a front-row seat as you watch God work in the lives of other people. This shared cause will further bond you and your spouse as you labor together for the kingdom.

THE GREENHOUSE EFFECT

As a married couple, we should never stop growing. We grow individually in our knowledge of Scripture and in our application of the truths we've learned. Our relationship with Christ deepens. We also grow as a couple, learning more about each other and hopefully strengthening our bond as husband and wife. And when we set out to find a mission unique to us as a couple, it opens up a whole new avenue for spiritual development.

This journey to discover our unique ministry niche helps us grow toward each other, not apart. Working alongside someone else toward a common goal develops one's camaraderie. We see this happen when a group embarks on a mission trip as a group of strangers but returns home as a circle of close friends. Coworkers develop solidarity. I've even seen parents of travel team baseball players—sitting on the sidelines of a sporting event for an entire summer—become dear friends. They not only cheer on the team but also work jointly, taking care of the transportation, the meals, and the housing of the team in hotels.

Working together on something that is designed solely to benefit others also benefits your marriage. And it helps you see why God put you two crazy kids together in the first place. You are a unique blend of two individuals not found anywhere else, a crew that can experience an exciting ministry God has tailor-made for you, one that will bless others and point them to Jesus.

What a blast it is to see how you as a couple can reach people you normally wouldn't influence by yourself. This team takes both a Mr. and a Mrs. It is not a solo act.

My friend Liz Curtis Higgs and her husband, Bill, form such a lineup. Whether they're working together in their ministry, where Liz writes and speaks while Bill manages the day-to-day operations of such a ministry, or together as they serve locally in their church and town, they blend their gifts, talents, and passions into one power-packed ministry team. This combo is described perfectly by Bill, who says, "I've always maintained that a marriage should create an entity that is bigger than the two individual participants . . . In other words, Bill and Liz ought to be something more than Bill by himself or Liz by herself. I think we've managed to accomplish that on some level."[1]

Are you ready to believe this about your own marriage? That the two of you together can serve God and others in a remarkable way that you couldn't do alone?

Good! Then get ready to write out that reality. Find yourself a cute notecard you can prop up at your desk or place on your dashboard. Or write it on the chalkboard in your kitchen or make it the lock screen message on your phone. Keep this thought before your eyes to remind you that you're a team. I'll write it here, making it specific to my marriage. You jot it down using your own names. Ready?

Todd + Karen = Ministry Team Us!

Yay, Team You! (I mean plural *you* as in *you all*. Oh, let's just make this easy and say, *Yay, Team Y'all!*)

Wait. Where was I? Oh, yes. Your team.

Your husband-wife dynamic duo is a ministry force to be reckoned with, a tool God can use to reach out to others and better their lives and improve your communities. I know there have been many famous husband-wife pairs where it seemed only one person was actually doing ministry. For example, when you think of the late Billy Graham, you may think of a preacher sharing the gospel all over the world. But his wife, Ruth, played an important part in the pairing that God used here in ministry on earth.

Ruth counseled people at Billy's crusades, wrote books and poetry, and became a Bible study partner and confidante to many in their wide circle of friends, including a few first ladies. Billy himself said about her, in a statement announcing her death in

2007, "Ruth was my life partner . . . We were called by God as a team. No one else could have borne the load that she carried."[2]

I can think of other couples who formed a team and discovered their own specific ministry in the process. Some were more public. Others seemed to merge quietly into the background but had a great and lasting impact nonetheless.

I think of a couple in their late twenties who opened their home for the youth of my church when I was in high school. The wife provided tasty teen-approved food, a fun sense of humor, and a shoulder to cry on when I needed advice. The husband loved to be outdoors and led many camping and boating trips for our gang. These excursions enabled us to get away from civilization for a while, open up emotionally, and talk about matters of faith. Both of them taught us the Bible. Both of them loved us unconditionally, even when we made poor decisions or got ourselves into trouble.

I recall another couple whose ministry looked very different. They didn't stand up front and teach; instead, they steadily served in the background, setting up others for success in their ministry endeavors. This couple took it upon themselves to pray for the various ministries at church, often coming to the church building when an activity was happening and sitting together in a closed classroom, praying for the event in progress. They came in early to set up chairs or stayed late to put them all away, sweep the floors, take out the trash, and turn off the lights as they left.

One "Ministry Team Us" may feel called to ministry in the local school, encouraging teachers and helping with the activities. Another may teach a group of toddlers every Sunday morning while their parents attend the worship service, so they show up each week ready to read stories, serve snacks, and change diapers, even though their own kids are no longer this small. (Now, *that's* a calling—wielding baby wipes when you don't have to! Major props to these peeps.) In each ministry team scenario, each spouse is afforded the opportunity to not only forge an effective team but also grow in maturity in their relationship with, and in their affection for, each other.

As a team, you will see up close each other's strengths and non-strengths. This isn't a bad thing. In fact, quite the opposite! It can lead to you becoming skilled at how to play to each other's strengths and to work on your own areas that need improvement. And all the while, you'll discover how your differences as individuals weave nicely together, covering over each other's flaws and forming the strong fabric of your marital team. You will also come to see your spouse's differences as assets.

My friend Ashleigh Slater, author of *Team Us*, said of her and her husband, Ted, "We're finding that as we band together for the common good of our relationship, instead of focusing on the places where we feel disappointed or our likes rejected, it becomes easier for us to remember to appreciate, not despise, the other's uniqueness. You know, that uniqueness that drew us to each other in the first place. The interesting thing is that as we've sought to do this, those differences have helped forge a confidence, or a 'thick skin,' in our marriage. It's a confidence that's left us comfortable enough with each other that we aren't threatened by diversity."[3]

> *Love is letting her charge her phone first. Marriage is buying a second charger.*
> *Spotted on sweatshirt*

CREATING YOUR OWN "MINISTRY TEAM US"

Let's say you sense what God is calling you as a couple to do. (Don't worry if you haven't yet. We'll walk through some steps for doing this in a bit.) You and the Mr. determine that your "Ministry Team Us" is to work with the local shelter for women-at-risk. How might that play out?

Well, your individual skill set looks like this:

You love to bake. You have a great listening ear. And you
       enjoy doing Bible studies and reading devotions.
Your husband is quite the handyman. He's also quite adept
       at being goofy and loves playing with kids.

Both of you desire to share the gospel, help alleviate suffering, and welcome people who are often marginalized. When you create a zip drive of your combined qualities and passions, a stellar team emerges. Together you can be a powerful presence and a huge blessing to your local women's shelter.

Here's how it might unfold:

You'll both volunteer to spend one or two evenings per month at the shelter. Because they serve the women a hot meal each evening, you'll bring along one of your delicious baked goods for dessert. You will both help serve the meal, and then you'll clear the tables as the workers prepare to hold the women's study time. During this time, your husband is on deck to keep the kids entertained by offering them one of his famous horsey rides or amusing them with his knee-slapping knock-knock jokes.

You will teach the evening's short lesson and then be available to talk one-on-one with any of the women who need a listening ear or someone to pray for them.

While the study hour is going on in one part of the shelter, your husband can be using his handyman skills to tinker around the shelter—tightening the loose hinge on the fridge, securing the handrail on the outside steps, or even performing routine household chores like cleaning the bathroom or taking out the trash.

What a huge benefit this will be to the shelter and what a blessing to the women who live there. As a side bonus, you and your husband will discover the thrill of performing a labor of love for the Lord shoulder to shoulder. Trust me. These evenings spent serving will do more to grow your love for each other than a typical date night will.

The possibilities are endless for what mission God has in mind for you and your spouse. Unearthing this mission is an elating venture. If you have kids, it only adds to the excitement as they too can be in on the action. (During a season when Todd and I volunteered at a homeless shelter, our young kids were able to come and help serve food at suppertime, and then they played with the children too.)

Your calling as a couple may be opening your home to foster children. Or simply opening your home to your neighbors. It may be performing physical work together at a nonprofit organization in your area. Or how about working locally and lovingly to bring about justice for, and inclusion of, those who are marginalized in your community? You may feel called to work with youth at church or the elderly at a nearby nursing home. But just how do you decide what your mission is? I'm going to pose a series of questions that can help you drill down deep, zeroing in on it. However, before you do that, I want to offer two simple suggestions to help you recognize your calling. First . . .

Look for the Pain

Our ears are often shut to the heart cries and heartaches of others; our eyes do not perceive their pain. We go about our days flitting from task to task, often dragging our children along for the ride. But who are we walking past in our quest to get life done? We are often passing people in pain. I was once told by a Bible study leader that if I ever felt purpose was missing from my life—or when I sized up my existence, even as a Christian, and it seemed rather boring—that it probably was due in part to the fact that I was not involved in the lives of people in pain.

Pain doesn't always mean something grave such as sex trafficking, abuse, or the sting of racism or discrimination. It can be so much subtler:

- the pain of loneliness felt by single people who have recently moved to your area because they lack any real connection with others beyond coworkers
- the pain of dashed hopes experienced by young couples facing infertility
- the pain of isolation felt by parents who are raising children with special needs
- the pain of feeling forgotten experienced by those who are elderly and live alone

Looking for people in pain may prompt you and your husband to begin brainstorming ways to reach out to them, lessening their sorrow, disappointment, or isolation. It also does something else for you. It's a lesson I learned from my mother back when I was in middle school.

One day after school, I sat at our dining room table, munching Fritos and telling my mom my current troubles. You know, the typical middle school drama—like having been left out of the circle of friends or failing to score an invitation to the latest slumber party of a girl in the popular crowd. I really can't remember exactly what it was. But I do remember my mother's response. She told me that if I ever feel like my life isn't going well and circumstances are causing me to feel down in the dumps, I need to stop and remember something. "There's always someone out there who has it worse off than you," she stated. "Go find that someone and do something to make their day. Somehow it'll make yours as well."

My mom was so right. I can look back over many decades and recall incidents where, instead of feeling sorry for myself, I located someone who had a harder hill to climb than I did, and so I devised something to cheer them up. I can still hear her words reverberating in my mind anytime now when I need a refresher course in this area. "Get your eyes off yourself, honey." Such great advice. Encouraging someone in physical, emotional, or financial distress helps to recalibrate our attitudes and teaches us to be thankful for all that we have. So, be on the lookout for that person, and then go and make his or her day.

Look for Your Old Self

The second thing that can be a great starting point in unearthing your mission as a couple is for both of you to look back over your life at the challenges and struggles you personally faced. Then go find your old self—reach out to them and spread a little kindness their way, living out the gospel as you do.

This notion led to a season when my husband and I opened our home to teenagers, quite a few of whom were from broken homes or living with a single parent. This was the case for me when I was in middle school and high school, being raised by a mom who suddenly found herself single. I had families in my life who opened their homes, their refrigerators, and, most importantly, their hearts. They also opened up the Bible to me.

For the last five years, our home has often been filled with teenagers, many of them being raised by single parents, or several who travel back and forth between the homes of their mothers and fathers. They've spent the night. They've played video games. Or they've watched a movie or sporting event on our TV. They've ransacked our pantry and raided our refrigerator, dunking dozens of cookies in about a gazillion gallons of milk. We wanted our house to feel like a second home to these teens.

When they felt free to flop on our couch, they also felt free to open up and talk. We had the joy and privilege of processing life with many of them. We've been able to sit with them and share about Jesus with some of them. And we've continued to follow them as they've graduated from high school and gone off to college or started working full-time. And we've had the immense joy of seeing two of them just recently give their lives to Jesus and be baptized. We pray that for all of them, the simple times spent within our four walls, feeling welcomed and loved, will be part of their voyage of faith one day.

What comes to your mind when you think of the phrase "look for your old self"? For many married folks, their thoughts migrate back to their days before they walked down the aisle.

Singles often feel left out—even at church. Actually, most often at church! We have developed a way of speaking about singleness that makes it seem subpar spiritually, implying that real life starts when you marry and fulfill God's only purpose for you—being hitched to your significant other. When I speak of God having a purpose for marriage, I am *never* implying that God's purpose is for everyone to be married! Singles are every bit as important in the body of Christ as their married brothers and sisters. In fact, they are even uniquely positioned to do things someone who is coupled can't (1 Corinthians 7:32–34). Author and blogger Jasmine Holmes made an insightful—and true—claim when she declared on Twitter, "Singleness isn't introductory level Christianity and marriage isn't an advanced course. We all stand on equal footing before the Bridegroom."[4]

Could your calling be to spend time with singles, remembering back to what you would have loved someone to have done for you during that season of life? Maybe there's a younger single you know from work or church who lives in an apartment without a laundry facility so she has to use a local—and lonely—laundromat. Invite her to come over and use your washer and dryer once a week while you share a cup of coffee with her or while she brings her laptop to catch up on email—something she can't do at the laundromat because it doesn't have Wi-Fi. But don't stop there. Enfold her into your family. Invite her for Sunday suppers or a barbecue in the backyard. Remember her on her birthday with a phone call or even a home-baked cake.

This "look for your old self" mission of kindness will send the blessings flying in both directions, and you'll make new friends in the process.

DISCERNING OUR CALLING AS A COUPLE

Look for people in pain. Check. Look for your old self. Check. These are both great starting points. But what else is there to consider?

Grab your hubby and get alone. No, not for a little romantic rendezvous. (You can do that later.) You may want to go to a coffee shop. Swing through a drive-through for some iced tea and go find a bench at the park. Drop the kiddos at grandma and grandpa's place and head back home, where it's finally quiet. (Just step over the toys and ignore the dirty dishes as you do.) Then take your time to work your way through these questions, discussing them in detail and recording your answers in a journal. For convenience, these questions are also listed again in the back on page 219 for you to photocopy if you'd like, with space to write down your answers. Then you and your husband can each have a copy to ponder, pray about, and write notes on.

1. Are there any areas in life where you feel you already have a ministry together? If so, what are they?

2. List any people or groups of people you know in your church or community who are in pain—physically, emotionally, relationally, or financially. Then look back over what you wrote and try to think of at least one way you can help each person or group you mentioned.

3. When you think of the concept of "finding your old self," what ideas for ministry come to mind?

4. Each of you list three to five interests you have that could lead you to a ministry. Then list some ways this passion or hobby might be used to help others (for example, you love to work in the yard, mowing the lawn or weeding your flower beds—perhaps you could have a summertime ministry doing this for an elderly couple at church who can still live alone in their home but can no longer perform outdoor maintenance).

5. Could any of the areas you listed above be something the two of you could do together? If so, which ones and how could both of you be a part?

6. In what ways could you use your home for ministry?

7. How might you use any items you own for ministry—your car, your washer and dryer, your lawn mower, or any tools you own?

8. If you have children, how could you incorporate them into one of the possible ministries you have mentioned?

9. What is one action step you can take to make a trial run at one of the ideas you've discussed above? Put a reminder on your phone or in your calendar app to revisit this, and make sure you follow through on it.

Don't expect a ta-da moment of instant revelation as you try to figure out what your mission in life is. It's a gradual process of clarification. It may take a while. And over the years, it may change. Some couples serve in the same area for forty years. Others switch it up several times over the course of one decade. Just start with these questions and revisit them as needed.

But first and always, make your mission a matter of prayer.

Pray about it separately. Pray about it together. Expect answers from God—and confirmation from each other—about what your next move is in your quest to discover your marriage's mission and ministry.

This has not been an exhaustive, perfect exercise in finding your ministry. It's just a springboard to help you begin a dialogue about finding your calling as a couple. Reexamine this list often in the following weeks, continuing to pray that God will clearly reveal to you what you as a team are called to do as you labor side by side serving others.

SUPPORTING EACH OTHER'S ENDEAVORS

When exploring the idea of finding a mission as a couple, you may also discover that one of you has interests and passions your spouse doesn't share. This is not only okay; it's also beneficial. Some marriages suffer because the couples have drifted apart, no longer sharing any common interests or spending much time together. However, there is a detrimental flip side to this too.

As Christians we often hear of the concept of oneness in marriage. Oneness is the idea that, when we marry, we are spiritually and physically united with our spouse. We are no longer two, but one. We see Jesus himself speak of this, when he connected one day with a religious leader who quizzed him on the topic of divorce: "Haven't you read . . . that at the beginning the

Creator 'made them male and female,' and said, 'For this reason a man will leave his father and mother and be united to his wife, and the two will become one flesh'? So they are no longer two, but one flesh. Therefore what God has joined together, let no one separate" (Matthew 19:4–6).

What a beautiful and profound thought—that of being one with your spouse. However, sometimes we can take oneness too far, assigning a definition to it that it's not meant to have. I've watched this taken-to-the-extreme categorization wreak havoc on a spouse—usually the wife.

Oneness does not mean that a spouse ceases to be an individual. It isn't meant to strip someone of their interests, their personality, their desires. Becoming one certainly does not mean that a wife is now the servant of the husband—or even of the entire family, should children be a part of the mix. She doesn't cease to be a separate being, merely melding into her husband's world and leaving behind any indications of her former self.

I've seen women wrongly buy into—or even be forced into—this line of thinking, sometimes of their own accord but often due to the pressure of their husband or faith community. They mistake *oneness* for *sameness*. They drop their interests, basically losing any identity that doesn't have to do with being a wife and mother.

One of two things usually happens. They strike a martyr's pose, not only becoming proud of how they don't do anything for themselves or take on any tasks that don't have to do with their families, but they also pressure others by arguing that it's the only biblical way to live. Or they adopt this family-only-no-more-me way of living begrudgingly. In both cases, often when the kids grow up and leave the home, these women chuck their husbands—and sometimes the church—and go off to finally do something for themselves for once. I have personally known about a half dozen women who sadly have done so.

In your quest to find your ministry as a couple, don't lose yourself. Don't let your husband lose himself either (although more often I sense it's a wife who is in peril of doing so). Yes, you are a couple, but you are also separate individuals. Mysteriously one, but also two individual souls.

During the time period when Todd and I "got married in a fever, hotter than a pepper sprout" (sorry, now my love of Johnny and June is showing!), lighting what is called a unity candle was popular, and so we elected to make it part of our ceremony. In this custom, the bride and groom each take a lit taper candle and together use the combined flames to light a bigger pillar candle and blow the taper candles out, symbolizing that they are no longer two but one. When discussing this part of the ceremony before we got married, my normally quiet I-have-no-opinion-in-the-matter fiancé piped up, "Hey, I have an idea. Let's light the pillar candle but let's not blow out our own. Let's put them back in their holders still burning. We're going to be Mr. and Mrs. Ehman, but we'll still be Todd and Kit too." (My college nickname, in case you didn't know.)

Remember, although your husband is now a Mr., he's still in there. You're still in there. Give each other space, as time allows, for your own hobbies, friends, and interests. Sure, spend time working on your relationship. But don't forget to go be an interesting person too—with pursuits that are all your own.

When a husband or wife encourages their spouse to take a painting class or an organic gardening seminar, to take up photography or rock climbing, or join a book club or nature center, it is both a selfless and self-assured thing—selfless because you're giving them room to explore an interest, and self-assured because this in no way threatens you personally or your oneness as a couple. You can even find pleasure in seeing them serve in a ministry you either don't have an interest in or don't have time to pursue.

Here is what ministry looks like right now in our family. (I give it just as an example, not for you to think you need to emulate.) I'm informally mentoring a young wife and new mother. I say *informally* because we aren't following a specific Bible study program. We just hang out together, and she asks me questions or bounces ideas off me. I have committed to not only spend time with her but to pray for her weekly. (I'd say daily, but I'd probably be lying!) I also love to bake or make meals for grieving families, those who've just welcomed a baby, or anyone else God lays on my heart.

Todd does a Bible study once a month or so with a coworker who is not a Christian but who is curious about spiritual matters and wants to learn more about the Bible. He also meets weekly with a second-grade boy through the partnership of our church and Kids Hope USA, a mentoring matchup organization that pairs a church member with an at-risk youth. They spend one hour together each Friday at the school, and Todd helps him with homework or plays some sort of educational game with him. Mostly, Todd just listens to and encourages him.

As a couple, we've committed to opening up our home to teens and young adults—mostly our kids' friends. However, we're considering serving in our church's college ministry, since one of our church's four venues meets on a local state university's campus for worship each weekend.

So we serve alone. We also do ministry together. I pray for him as he heads off to mentor his young friend or to open up the Bible with his coworker over a cup of coffee—in both instances occasionally sending along one of my homemade treats. Todd also prays for me and—the best part—cleans up the kitchen and washes the dishes after I've baked up a storm making a treat for someone. (I love a man with dishpan hands!)

When we're expecting company, we work together to get the house to a comfortable, lived-in, but mostly clean state. I dust. He vacuums. He swings by the store to pick up snacks. I put the coffee on and keep the conversation going with our guests during their stay. (Not a huge feat since I can talk for a whole hour with no topic!)

Working side by side with your spouse while allowing each other to have their own pursuits and service goals helps you see each other as more than just a roommate or someone you rotate chores with. When I walk by our home office door, I may catch a glimpse of Todd prepping for his study with his friend from work or flipping through a brain-teaser book as he gets ready to spend time with his grade school mentee. It warms my heart and grows my affection for that makes-me-crazy-sometimes man.

And I'm reminded anew of the main reason we got hitched in the first place.

During our eight-month engagement, we started 150 days before our wedding day and read one psalm from the Bible each day, beginning with Psalm 150 and working our way backward. When we found ourselves at T minus 34 days, we also found our marriage verse! We'd known we wanted to serve God together; we just hadn't encountered this Scripture that stated our aim so well. It is Psalm 34:3: "Glorify the LORD with me; let us exalt his name together."

The word *glorify* in this verse—and elsewhere in Scripture—means "to make famous." We don't love and serve as a couple so we can draw attention to ourselves, so others think we're such wonderful people. We do it to make God become known to others as the wonderful, matchless, indescribable God that he is!

COUNTING THE COST

One last challenge: when you consider being a couple who seeks to minister together, know that it will be costly. It will cost time and effort. It will require communication and flexibility. And it can cost you financially—even taking some things away from your own wish list in order to cheer or encourage another soul.

Recently I was greatly challenged by a guest speaker one Sunday at church. I never wrote down his name—boo!—so I can't give him credit for the heart-searching question he asked our church that day.

He stated how we Americans spend so much money on ourselves but don't often think of spending money on others who are less fortunate than us. We certainly spend oodles of money on things not essential to our existence. And for some, the smallest portion of our budget goes to the direct funding of the spread of the gospel—an endeavor that can affect eternity in the lives of others. He challenged us to rethink where our money was going by uttering this sentence: "Will you dare to defer your dream kitchen in light of eternity?"

Ugh.

Well . . . guess what Todd and I were just about to do? Uh-huh—complete with a farm sink, a subway tile backsplash, and hickory hardwood floors. Now, I'm not attempting to detonate a guilt bomb and toss it your way if you *are* remodeling your kitchen. We may even do so one day—if we ever find a great deal on a mid-century brick ranch that has an original kitchen in desperate need of a makeover. The point is that our kitchen really doesn't need it. Our home is just ten years old. Our kitchen counters and cabinets are completely satisfactory—and only slightly outdated and a darker color than I now prefer. I'd probably just been watching too many "home renovation" shows and got it in my mind that I simply must have an HGTV-style, white-and-bright trendy kitchen too.

We changed our minds, left the money in the bank, and are praying about how it may be used to advance the gospel. We may give it away. We may save it for a renovation another day that is actually needed to make our home better suited for hospitality. Or maybe God will call us to put in a built-in pool so our church can use it for baptisms. (Okay—that's a stretch!)

A DELIGHTFULLY DULL VALENTINE'S DAY

As love matures and you form a ministry team with your spouse, God will allow you to see spiritual growth in your own life and in the life of your mate. But you will also get to witness the joy that comes when you as a team put others' interests before your own. This just happened to us a few weeks ago, and I can't stop smiling when I think of it!

Valentine's Day was fast approaching. Todd and I hadn't really done anything fancy at all on Valentine's Day for quite a few years. Usually something was going on at school or sports with one of the kids, or we just stayed home and sat in front of the fire, keeping warm in our cold Michigan winter. However, this year we had set aside a little bit of money to go out on a date, probably having dinner at someplace a tad bit more upscale than a chain restaurant, grabbing a movie, and then going out for coffee and dessert on the way home.

As we thought through our options for our outing, my mind couldn't help but keep migrating to my single friends. For many of them, Valentine's Day stinks. *Really* stinks. A few of them refer to it as Singles Awareness Day. They spend the day not with a significant other but with evidence of happy couples parading before their eyes all day long: social media posts of flowers and chocolates, gifts of jewelry shown to them by their friends from their boyfriends, and scads of flowers delivered to other women in their office while their desk sits mockingly empty, a constant reminder of their unattached status—which culture wrongly tells them means they are somehow "less than."

I was imagining that last upsetting scenario when God gave me a sudden brainstorm. I relayed the idea to Todd when he returned home from work, and he was totally on board. We set out to sneakily implement our plan. It took a little detective work and a few phone calls, but soon we were ready to roll.

With a little help from an office snitch, I came up with a list of the women who work for us in the office at Proverbs 31 Ministries who are unmarried and also unattached—sixteen of them, as it turned out. Since I work remotely from my home in Michigan and our office is in North Carolina, I identified a flower shop online that delivers to the town where our office is located. I called the shop and told them our desire to order sixteen single roses, each accompanied by baby's breath and greenery, and wrapped individually. Then I asked whether we would only be charged one delivery fee. (Hey, one can be generous and still a penny-pincher!)

When the woman asked me if she could be so nosy as to inquire what the flowers were for, I told her our idea. She was so touched that she knocked off a couple bucks from each bouquet, granting us a quantity discount deal. (Score!) Todd and I used the money we'd planned to spend on our night out on the town to pull off this cross-country shower of flowers instead.

With each of the roses, a note was tucked in that read, "You are loved and appreciated—by God and by us."

On Valentine's Day morning, I poured myself a cup of toasted coconut coffee and whispered a prayer to God, asking him to enable this "Sweet 16" group of spiritual sisters to know how very much they are treasured and loved.

Late in the morning, my phone began to ping and buzz with notifications. I received several private messages on Facebook and Instagram—as well as text messages and emails—from my coworkers who were the recipients of our bouquets of love that day. Some were giggling with delight. Others shed a tear.

Many of them said that when the florist showed up, they sorta sighed, knowing that none of the flowers were going to be for them. Then they nearly flipped when a bouquet was dropped off on their desks. One woman even emailed, stating how much she had dreaded going to work that morning. However, she also had whispered a prayer to God before she left her home, asking if he might send her some flowers that day, knowing he could if he wanted to. When she was given her gift, she just knew it came from Jesus himself.

Yes, it did.

I forwarded all the messages on to my husband at work. Both of us were tickled with glee at the joy these blossoms brought to our single friends on what otherwise might have been a day of dread.

For our romantic Valentine's date that night, we stayed home, enjoying our warmed-up leftovers eaten in front of the fire while watching reruns of *Shark Tank*. We also rejoiced in the peace and satisfaction that comes from listening to God, cooperating with him, and then standing back and watching him work. Cupid himself could not have planned a better way for us to spend the evening. It is now my all-time favorite memory of Valentine's Day.

Such joy and fulfillment are waiting for you and your husband as you also discover where God is calling you to serve him by serving others. Minister together. Also minister alone. Pray for each other. Chip in and help with the work of each other's calling. Share the labor in the unique ministry he has called both of you to as a couple.

Together you will fall deeper in love with each other as you form your own "Ministry Team Us" and touch lives for the kingdom of God.

The lives of others—and also your very own.

WHEN YOU'RE NOT SPIRITUALLY
IN SYNC

Perhaps you and your husband are not spiritually synced—
either because he is not a Christ follower, or he is but he's
not interested in growing spiritually. As I've walked alongside friends in this situation and also supported them in
prayer, I have observed a few principles that may help you
if you're in a spiritually out-of-sync marriage right now.
First . . .

**1. Realize his spiritual growth—or his salvation—is
not your responsibility.** You can't make your husband fully
follow Jesus. It just isn't part of your earthly job description.
God is the one who does the saving. And the day is coming—as it will for you and me someday—when your husband
will stand before the Lord to answer for what he did with
the call of the gospel while here on earth. Yes, it's your job
to preach the gospel with your behavior. Such preaching
does not include Bible-thumping, guilt-inducing lectures,
or backhanded comments about how he doesn't follow God.

**2. Don't buy the lie that God only works in the
relationships of two strong Christians.** God won't be
shoved into a box. He is all-knowing and all-powerful, and
nothing is too hard for him. You can trust him to show up in
your marriage, answering prayer and initiating change. Your
marriage can be a place where you see God at work daily.
Satan would want you to believe otherwise, become discouraged, and stop trying. Don't for a minute think God only

shows up when both spouses are committed believers. He is working everywhere, and we would do well to cooperate.

3. Don't preach. When we want so badly for someone we love to follow Jesus, our go-to plan is often to tell them to start doing so—and pronto! However, often even our sincerest concern comes across as self-righteous preaching. Romans 2:4 reads, "Do you show contempt for the riches of his kindness, forbearance and patience, not realizing that God's kindness is intended to lead you to repentance?" Our Father God's grace-filled kindness leads us to repentance. Not his lectures. Not his "you should" shaming. No . . . his *kindness*. So, zip your lips and demonstrate kindness in your behavior. Oh, you'll still talk. This next idea tells when and to whom.

4. Do pray. Use your words in prayer, asking God to guide your interactions with your husband and behave in a way that makes him want to know more about following God. Also, pray that your spouse will ask you about your faith, and then be ready to answer! The apostle Peter wrote, "In your hearts revere Christ as Lord. Always be prepared to give an answer to everyone who asks you to give the reason for the hope that you have. But do this with gentleness and respect" (1 Peter 3:15).

5. Treat him with the same respect you would show to a growing believer. This should go without saying, but I'm going to say it anyway because I've seen this happen—often. You are granted no right to treat him badly because he doesn't believe.

6. Don't mentally or verbally compare. My husband and I have listened to men tell just how it makes them feel—and how it sets them up for failure—when their wives talk about other men who are spiritually serious (especially in family life) when their husbands are not. This is in no way helpful, so just don't go there. Also, realize before the words come out of your mouth that when you compare, you are coveting. The tenth commandment tells us not to covet what our neighbor has—including their spouse (Deuteronomy 5:21). The Hebrew word for *covet* means "to desire," and it isn't just talking physically. We covet someone else's spouse when we wish our own was as spiritual as theirs.

7. Together find an area of service, or tag along on his hobby and find your own mission. Don't be discouraged, thinking you and your husband can't find a mission together—you can. Pray that you can open up a conversation with him about serving together to better your community, help out a charity, or serve an organization. If he's not interested, join him in one of his hobbies, tagging along and asking God to use you to minister to the people you meet along the way.

Your spouse's sluggish—or even absent—spiritual growth is concerning, for sure. However, don't let it prevent you from trusting God, from expecting him to work in your marriage, and from giving you lots of practice performing the important work of wordlessly preaching the gospel. As the apostle Peter wrote, "In the same spirit you married women should adapt yourselves to your husbands, so that even if they do not obey the Word of God they may be won to God *without any word being spoken*, simply by seeing the pure and reverent behavior of you, their wives" (1 Peter 3:1–2, Phillips, emphasis mine).

EIGHT

THE SETUP FOR SUCCESS

He is your friend who pushes you nearer to God.
ABRAHAM KUYPER

But woe to him who is alone when he falls,
for he has no one to help him up.
ECCLESIASTES 4:10 NKJV

Long before the days of video streaming, one of the ways I could get some alone time as the mom of three small children was to allow them to watch one of their favorite movies—*Mary Poppins*. The three of them would climb up on our couch and cuddle together under a throw blanket while I popped a VHS into the VCR. (Anyone remember VCRs? Anyone?) I'd head to the next room to sit at the kitchen table, sipping coffee while reading a book, writing letters, or just looking out the window doing nothing—something I rarely did.

Our home was very tiny. If I leaned my head back ever so slightly and peeked around the corner, the kids were within my sight and almost within reach. Still, I felt like I was getting a much-deserved break. And my brood was getting a real treat, watching Mary magically tidy up the toy room or Bert and the other chimney sweeps twirl around and leap about the rooftops of London. Of course, when that part of the movie materialized on screen, they had to try to "step in time!" right along with the singing and dancing men—all over our living room furniture!

Recently, I stumbled upon a link to a video someone had created and then posted on YouTube; it was a short collection of selected scenes from this same Disney classic. The strategic way they cut and spliced together only certain parts of the movie completely changed its look and feel. Dubbed *Scary Mary*, this recut version looks like a trailer for a horror film, with Mary sometimes peering out windows, or dark gloomy skies overshadowing the screen. And at one point, the children appear to be running for their lives! All the while, Mary's voice can be heard singing the words to one of the songs from the soundtrack, originally meant as a lullaby. To hear her slowly, almost inaudibly vocalize the words, "Stay awake, don't rest your head" was so creepy it made my skin crawl!

By choosing only the seemingly dark and dreary parts, the video creator was able to make you believe something totally untrue—that *Mary Poppins* isn't a delightful children's classic but a petrifying horror flick!

So, what does this clever string of clips have to do with marriage? Plenty. When thinking about our own marriage, we often *selectively* retrieve memories of events and interactions with our spouse, recalling only the worst of times. Then we string the "clips" together in a mash-up of memories that paint our marriages in a ghastly light!

Oh sure, we all have bad times in our marriages. Times of underlying tension. Heated conflicts. Cold shoulders. All-out domestic disagreements we'd classify as fights. We've experienced hurt feelings, dashed hopes, and seasons of intense sadness.

All of us! But we must not let our minds play tricks on us, fooling us into believing our entire marriage has been horrendous. We must not let our minds craft our own *Scary Marriage* movie, but we need to do these two things instead: (1) intentionally focus on—and be truly thankful for—the good times we've had and (2) learn to reframe the bad times in a fresh and different light.

FOCUS ON THE GOOD TIMES

Instead of looking only for the bad in our marriage, we can implement a powerful practice that will enable us to focus on what God is doing through *all* the portions of our marriage. What is that practice? Look for the good—and give thanks for it!

Now, I'll admit there are some people who just do this naturally. Think of two people with opposite perspectives out for a stroll on a spring afternoon. They walk by a flower garden completely overgrown with stubble and weeds. The first person views the drab brown and green foliage before her and announces, "Wow, what a mess! Look at all those weeds!"

Then the second person sauntering along looks at that same weedy patch. However, she decides to peer deeper. When she does, she spots one solitary, tiny flower barely poking its brilliant red head above the soil. She turns to her pessimistic friend and declares, "Yeah, but will you look at that gorgeous flower?"

We need to learn to do what our flower-spotting friend seems to do with ease—look for the lovely in the center of the thickets of life. This is part of what I think it means to have a childlike faith—one that displays earnest gratitude in even the simple parts of daily life.

Last summer, I was treated to lunch at my friend Lindsey's house, where we were joined by her four kiddos as we ate our tacos and fruit. Her youngest, five-year-old Coeburn, volunteered to thank God for our food that afternoon. We bowed our heads, eyes tightly shut. Except for Coeburn. He prayed, all right. However, I could tell he had at least one squinted eye open because, while offering grace, he thanked Jesus for every single item on the table, his raspy voice sweetly wafting toward heaven.

He matter-of-factly offered his prayer, saying, "Thank you, Jesus, for meat with taco seasonings, tortilla shells, lettuce, shredded cheddar cheese, tomatoes, peppers, Aldi potato chips, sliced apples, and the sour cream—uh . . . I mean the nonfat plain Greek yogurt."

What a hoot! When acknowledging God's provision for our meal, my little friend simply opened his eyes and thanked God for whatever he saw before him—whether he liked it or not. Not too sure many young boys get geeked over nonfat plain Greek yogurt.

Have you ever stopped to just think about your life for a moment? I don't mean the issues that are troubling you or the things you're worried about. I mean the things of life that are before your eyes daily, complete with ordinary taco dinners and your own share of nonfat yogurt. Yes, they are commonplace and repetitive. Some things may even be slightly sour. But when we consciously show gratefulness for even the common articles and happenings we typically take for granted, it switches our thinking, empowering us to not only display gratitude but feel it deep within our souls.

I'm embarrassed to admit that some days my prayer life looks like a long list of "gimmies"—*Give me this. Give me that.* Oh sure, maybe I thank God for "my many blessings," sweeping them all into a pious pile and then mentioning them during the perfunctory intro to my prayer—you know, before I get down to the *real* business of rattling off what I think I need and know I want.

But when I slowly and deliberately think through my life, I can honestly thank God for the often-overlooked riches my life contains:

- a home with heat
- running water
- enough food to feed my family
- clothing to wear
- products for our family's personal hygiene
- our cars—one with more than 200,000 miles on it and one not far behind
- the fact that no one in our family has major health issues
- education for my children
- friends and family members—even the difficult ones
- citizenship in a country that allows us to worship freely

When I take the time to be intentionally filled with gratitude, it lifts my spirits. And it makes me realize how very fortunate I am indeed. Sure, I don't live in the nicest house in my town, or even in my neighborhood. But I have a roof over my head. Our food isn't gourmet fancy, but it feeds us well. Our cars aren't eye-catching, but they do get my people safely from point A to point B. And I certainly praise God for freedom, especially when the latest world news updates crawl across the bottom of my television screen.

If we take the time to do the same thing with our marriages, the same feeling of gratefulness will wash over our souls. Every marriage is a unique blend of awesome and awful. However, we get to choose which aspect we'll dwell on. When we dwell on the awful, we craft our own horror flick and want to run away—or at least cover our eyes. But it doesn't have to be that way if we focus on the awesome instead.

Here's a little assignment for you. Stop what you're doing. Think back over your relationship for a moment. Intentionally ponder the awesome times in your marriage. Name the tremendous qualities in your spouse, not the troublesome ones.

Those characteristics about your guy you respect. If we look carefully at *any* person, we can find something about them that is praiseworthy. I can even do this with some of the most difficult people I know. Certainly we should be able to do it with our spouse.

Now, in all honesty, it's certainly easier to collect a long bullet-pointed list of all of our husband's faults and shortcomings. Let's tear up that mental list, okay? Instead—and I'm saying this in all seriousness—grab a paper and pen, the notes app on your phone, or even a leftover clean napkin from the pizza that was delivered last night and write down those traits unique to your husband so they are there before you in black-and-white. Once you do, you'll be reminded again of the reason you fell in love with your boyfriend-turned-betrothed, the assets about him that first attracted you and made you fall crazy and head over heels in love.

Every marriage is a unique blend of awesome and awful.

Gratefulness outmaneuvers our grumbling and parks our brains in a lovely place—where the flowers outshine the weeds.

Now, I know you may be thinking, *But we've had so many tumultuous times in our marriage!* From minor conflicts to all-out brawls. From slightly hurt feelings to a deeply wounded soul. Loss of trust. Loss of the feelings of love for each other. All the rotten ripples in your relationship.

I get it. Believe me, I do! In fact, were I to stop now and do just what I asked you to do above, but instead I only itemized the awfulness of my marriage rather than the awesomeness, I'd push myself right into a deep, blue funk and flop on the sofa to have a good cry (and probably down a bunch of dark chocolate while I did!). Even though I may not like Todd's backward-from-me way of looking at problems, I'm grateful it often brings to my mind an aspect of the situation that I wouldn't have thought of on my own.

Even though I usually interpret his decision-making process as "slow," it's actually a more thorough way of coming to conclusions than my quick-thinking and immediate-implementing habits. His careful and deliberate decision-making methods have saved us both money and heartache over the years.

We can choose to reframe the times of fight and frustration, to see the heat of conflict as something meant for evil that God can use for good instead. Think I'm crazy?

Hang with me now. You'll see.

REFRAME THE BAD TIMES

Once when I was making my way through airport security, I was stopped and pulled aside to have my carry-on roller bag searched. The machine that examines luggage had indicated that I might be carrying something considered a weapon. When my bag was carefully opened and the item retrieved, I discovered that the article they thought might be dangerous was my worn leather Bible. And you know what? They were right—but not in a physically destructive sort of way.

Our Bible can be a powerful weapon, enabling us to apply its truths and learn its lessons, one of which is that even the not-so-great times in life can be used for good by God. This has been especially true for me when it comes to those not-so-great times in our marriage: the days I felt lonely or misunderstood; the nights I was fuming mad over something Todd had done—or even had failed to do; the days we clashed with and lashed out at each other; the times I royally blew it and behaved in a manner that was the exact opposite of how I, as someone who claims to follow Jesus, should behave.

The hard realities of marriage should drive us to God's Word for comfort, clarity, solutions, and even sanity. And God's Word often encourages us to communicate with God in prayer—not in a saintly and safe way, reciting eloquent words and pious platitudes, but by falling on our faces in desperation, begging for help. At those nearly unbearable places in our marriage, we empathize with President Abraham Lincoln, who once admitted, "I have been driven many times upon my knees by the overwhelming conviction that I had nowhere else to go."[1]

However, the bright side is that these times of trouble in marriage can be the exact place where God meets us in our despair and teaches us what it means to suffer, survive, and grow spiritually stronger because of it all. Billy Graham once observed, "Mountaintops are for views and inspiration, but fruit is grown in the valleys."[2] God is able to produce the fruit of the Spirit in you—love, joy, peace, patience, kindness, goodness, faithfulness, gentleness, and self-control—when you let him work on refining your faith, even in the spiritual valleys (Galatians 5:22–23).

Grab hold of a new perspective: these awful times can also be awe-filled times. You will look back in awe someday as you see how your spiritual growth spiked when your marriage hit a low, when you too were driven to your knees because you had nowhere else to go. Your communication with God during these times of anxious prayer will allow you to become spiritually synced with him as he shows you answers through his Word. Your relationship with him will deepen as you understand more clearly what it means to walk in faith.

The grace of God will train you in righteousness.

The goodness of God will prompt you to act in kindness, even when you are wronged.

The wisdom of God will provide you with answers and direction.

The power of God will embolden you to act on those answers and go in the given direction.

The forgiveness of God will inspire you to, in turn, forgive your spouse.

And the steadfastness of God will empower you to keep showing up and keep walking in faith.

When you are serious about walking with Jesus, he will show you how to be thankful for the difficulties of marriage. Even when you can't see how those difficulties are stretching and shaping your faith right now, trust that they are drawing you closer to God. Drawing closer to God doesn't just affect your relationship with Jesus; it betters the one with your husband too, causing you to love and desire him more.

I have learned to reframe the frustrations I have with my husband by deciding first of all to stop thinking they are no longer going to happen. Just logging in years—even decades—in your marriage doesn't mean you'll come to a place where you're no longer exasperated with your spouse at times. The key is to stop looking at the frustration and start looking for the growth.

God has grown my patience because of my marriage. He has taught my husband to speak up more often. He has taught me to back off and stop badgering when we face conflict. And both of us have learned that each other's weaknesses—I mean *non-strengths*—are part of a package deal. They are no surprise to God. After all, he made us!

When we grant each other the freedom to be ourselves and focus on our own growth rather than on trying to make the other person change, God often changes our hearts. I know it sounds crazy, but I'm actually thankful for all aspects of my husband's makeup—quirks, personality differences, non-strengths and all! That is, as long as I don't let them rub me the wrong way but instead smooth off any rough edges I have in my own personality.

My friend Jennifer blogs about marriage at her site *Unveiled Wife*. She writes in her book of the same name, "Drawing closer to God has radically influenced my life. Over the years, I slowly began recognizing the positive changes in my husband and me, knowing without a doubt it was God's presence in our lives as we submitted to Him that was positively affecting our relationship. Each and every transformation added to the development of our characters to be more like Christ, which made us become all the more attracted to each other in the process."[3]

Drawing closer to God takes time. And disappointments. But facing our disappointments with courage and learning from them bring us hope. Hopeful faith sustains us during the silent gaps in our spiritual timelines—those barren white spaces where we can't see God at work. When we possess faith, we aren't always clear on what God is doing. Yet we can cling to this observation of author Philip Yancey: "What is faith, after all, but believing in advance what will only make sense in reverse."[4]

The dark times in marriage are like Holy Saturday—that dark day that was suspended between the Friday Jesus died on the cross and the Sunday when he arose. It may feel lonely and confusing, but if we cleave to God and his Word, we will be able to experience Psalm 30:5 in a mighty way: "Weeping may stay for the night, but rejoicing comes in the morning."

So, get ready to be vulnerable, even disappointed at times. Disappointment comes with the territory of marriage. C. S. Lewis famously maintained:

> To love at all is to be vulnerable. Love anything, and your heart will certainly be wrung and possibly be broken. If you want to make sure of keeping it intact, you must give your heart to no one, not even to an animal. Wrap it carefully round with hobbies and little luxuries; avoid all entanglements; lock it up safe in the casket or coffin of your selfishness. But in that casket—safe, dark, motionless,

airless—it will change. It will not be broken; it will become unbreakable, impenetrable, irredeemable.[5]

Yes, love hurts. But we as believers can bring our hurts to Jesus, who identifies with us and holds us ever close when we traipse through life's summits and swamps. And we must also recognize that even the most skilled climbers know a very important rule—never hike alone.

Marching through marriage with a close friend or two right by your side can help you maintain a "keep showing up" attitude in your own marriage. Have you made a point to pray for, support, encourage, and help better the marriages of other friends you know? Have you asked others to do the same for you? It's time that the church fought for marriages from within, doing all we can to point others to Jesus.

It is time we set up a safety net.

WE NEED MORE SPOTTERS

"We need more spotters!" I called to the girls on my cheerleading squad. We were attempting to build a new mount, one in which the girl on the top of the pyramid would be tossed into the air before being caught in the arms of two of her teammates standing on the ground. Before making that dismount, however, she had to successfully get to the top of the mount. And so I called for more spotters.

A spotter is someone on the ground who stands ready, arms outstretched, to assist the gal on top should she start to wobble. If she does, the spotter reaches up and holds her ankles to steady her and keep her on course. The spotters on the ground are essential to the success of the mount. They can make or break the landing. They can prevent falls and ultimately injuries.

The sideline of a football game isn't the only place where we need spotters. We need them in our lives as Christians as well. We must surround ourselves with those who will look out for our good, with arms outstretched, ready to steady us should we begin to falter.

> *I love you no matter what you do, but do you have to do so much of it?*
>
> Jean Illsley Clarke

A little more than a decade ago, Todd and I were the facilitators of a small group of couples who met together for a Bible study on the topic of marriage. There was quite a cross section of couples in our group. Several had been married for ten to twenty years. Of those people, most were in their first marriage, but a few were in their second. There was one couple who had just celebrated their forty-fifth anniversary. And there was also a couple who had walked down the aisle barely six months before. For the husband it was his first marriage. For the wife it was her second. All in all, there were eight couples—all of whom seemed well-adjusted, happily hitched, and committed to having their marriage sync up with Scripture. And today?

Half of those couples are no longer married to each other. Half!

Todd and I often wonder just what went wrong.

Sadly, over the quarter century we've been married, my husband and I have witnessed the failure of not only these fellow small group members, but of more than a dozen or so marriages of friends, fellow church members, and extended family.

Looking back, we can see the warning signs that some of these people were beginning to wobble, to flirt with the devil, and to invite trouble—and ultimately infidelity—into their lives. This left us pondering the question, *Could we have done something to help?* We also contemplated, *What can we do as a couple to prevent something like this from happening to us?*

In my happily-ever-after way of thinking, I used to believe that Christians never had affairs or divorced. Unfortunately, over the years we have witnessed many genuine, godly believers who became victims of divorce. They meant their marriage vows and intended to keep them "till death," but their mate decided to forsake their vows. Sometimes a spouse's double life was discovered. Or abuse was part of the picture, leaving them with no other option than to leave.

While this has sometimes been the case, more often than not, what we've witnessed are marriages where one partner lets down their guard and allows a casual acquaintance to crescendo into a full-blown affair. Many of these marriages were ones we thought were going along quite nicely. Well-adjusted kids. Stable home. Positions on the PTO or church board. What on earth happened? In part . . .

They had no spotters.

The unfaithful partners in each of these cases were islands unto themselves. Yes, they showed up for church. They looked and acted fine and faithful. But they made a chain of decisions unchallenged by others that landed them in the arms—and eventually the beds—of someone who was not their spouse. Then the horrible aftermath of the divorce took its devastating toll on all those around them.

While many say that divorce is the business of only the two parties involved, my husband and I look at it differently. We've told our kids that divorce is like the atomic bomb that was dropped on Hiroshima. While it was aimed only at the target in the crosshairs in the scope, lives for miles around and generations afterward have been affected by its dropping. These affairs and resulting divorces have shattered the lives of their children and have saddened neighbors, extended families, and coworkers. These splits have left other kids, watching from a distance, wondering if their own parents will call it quits too.

Looking back at a couple of these situations, my husband and I can remember times when we felt a check in our spirit about the behavior of some of these people. We were uncomfortable with the attention they gave to a member of the opposite sex or with their minor obsession with a fellow sports parent. We even spotted a few out in public with someone who was not their spouse, nor someone with whom they had a business or other legitimate connection, but we chose to say nothing. Looking back now, we wish we had, in love, risked the loss of friendship or the possibility of being misunderstood. We lost these people as friends anyway when they decided to leave their families for someone else.

So, what can we do? Can we prevent this from happening in the lives of others? Not always. However, we can take precautions to make sure we have our own spotters in place.

I have a friend whom I will tell immediately if I'm having any improper thoughts about another man. Maybe I enjoy the company or the verbal praise of a male a little too much. Or it may be as innocent as my thinking, *Boy, I wish Todd liked talking current events and politics with me like so-and-so does*, or *So-and-so is such an attentive husband—and he isn't forgetful, like someone I know.* Comparing our spouse to others lets Satan have a foothold. Before too long, he has us in a no-holds-barred chokehold.

This accountability arrangement with my friend works both ways. In one instance, she admitted to me her improper thoughts about a man and her excitement about seeing him in a church committee situation. That was all it took to extinguish the flicker before it combusted and became a blaze. After confessing her thought patterns to me, her feelings for him went away.

Secrecy often breeds sin.

Wrong choices also can become the breeding ground for sin. In each of the heartbreaking situations we've witnessed, it was a series of increasingly detrimental choices that led to the breakup of the marriage. In one instance, a wife started to frequent a certain business establishment. No bad choice there. But she then made the choice to talk repeatedly and flirtatiously with some married men there. Next, she chose to spend time alone with one man in particular. One day, she allowed physical contact to occur. This spiraled out of control and led to an all-out physical affair. Before long, two marriages ended in divorce, affecting more than a half dozen innocent children! And all it took was a series of four bad choices in a row.

Listen to me. Please! We are *all* capable of four bad choices in a row. Of four bad choices that can wreak havoc on our marriages. *All* of us—me included.

I never assume I have a guarantee that my marriage will last. Oh, I pray it will. I work toward doing my part to make it happen. But I am ever cognizant of the reality that it takes two people to make a great marriage, but it takes only one of them to break it up. That "one of them" could be me.

I don't say this just to make myself look relatable. I say it because I've known a few couples—they were extremely close to us—who I never dreamed would be the ones whose marriages would collapse, ending up in divorce court. However, all of them did so because of a short—but very destructive—series of choices one of the spouses made.

Our life itself is a series of choices. We don't always choose what is best. We sin. We rationalize. We refuse to admit fault. We may think we are standing strong with certain lines drawn in the sand, lines we vow we will never cross. But slowly—over time—our rationalizations, our stubborn bent to sin that is not tempered by confession and repentance, our assertion that marriage should make us happy yet we don't *feel* happy—all of these combine, inching the line a little farther away.

So yeah, we keep our vow to never cross the line. We *don't* ever cross it.

We just relocate it to a new spot.

Having a safety net of Christian friends can help us choose wisely more often. And they give us a safe place to process, as well as a community of welcome for the times when we blow it. And trust me—there will be times when you still blow it. (I have my closest friends on speed dial for just such times!)

To help ensure that we make choices that are in keeping with God's will, we all need a spotter or two. They can help keep our wobble from becoming an all-out free fall.

SETTING UP YOUR SAFETY NET

So, what does this look like in real life? Well, that is where you start . . . *in real life*—often abbreviated when posting online as "IRL." Contrast that with another abbreviation commonly used today—"URL." URL is an abbreviation that stands for Universal Resource Locator. This means a web address, the letters or words you type into your internet browser when you want to navigate to a certain site.

Online resources can be encouraging and effective. There are plenty out there that can help you in your relationship with your husband. I hope the spaces and places where I post content and share my thoughts online assist others and enhance their spiritual lives. But caution is needed. We can't let URL trump IRL. We need people in real life with whom we can honestly share about our marriages. People who see us in our day-to-day ordinary life rather than only viewing our smiling profile pictures on our social media accounts.

I've seen a troublesome trend as I've watched a shift taking place. We've taken the pixilated images and typed-from-afar words on our assorted screens and substituted them for flesh-and-blood friends. This is not a helpful trend. It's so easy to be someone online that you really are not in real life. Oh, we may type or text words that seem authentic and vulnerable, yet still be hiding who we really are. IRL personal friends can keep this dichotomy from happening.

We need friendships with people who see us interact with our husband. We especially need a close connection with at least one friend with whom we can drop our guard. This is more crucial than having many online friends we know only at a surface level or because we clicked the "Follow" button on their social media accounts.

If at all possible, work toward setting up the following safety nets in your life:

- a few close female friends who have the same goal of making their marriages healthy and God-honoring
- a couple with whom you and your mate regularly hang out and process life
- one trusted friend who will serve as your locked box, with whom you can openly and honestly share

Let's think about your small safety-net circle of friends.

Friendships are necessary in life. However, they can be either an asset or a liability when it comes to your thoughts about and actions in your marriage.

We are born craving connection with other humans. God gives us guidelines in the Bible for what our friendships should look like. Throughout its pages, snippets of Scripture give us both the benefits of having close friends and the warnings about what type of close companions to avoid.

Here are just a few truths about friendship, along with the verses where we find them.

- The character of the friends you pick can either help you grow in wisdom or tempt you with foolishness that can bring about a damaging outcome: "Walk with the wise and become wise, for a companion of fools suffers harm" (Proverbs 13:20).

- A friend may see aspects of a situation you can't see, because they are looking from the outside in. Their advice for action can often be better than a plan you come up with yourself: "Oil and incense bring joy to the heart, and the sweetness of a friend is better than self-counsel" (Proverbs 27:9 CSB).

- A godly friend can keep you from making rash and foolish decisions in marriage you might make if you don't ask for someone else's opinion of the situation: "The way of fools seems right to them, but the wise listen to advice" (Proverbs 12:15).

- Here are two Scriptures where we see warnings about what type of friends you should—and should not—choose: "Do not be misled: 'Bad company corrupts good character'" (1 Corinthians 15:33). And "The righteous choose their friends carefully, but the way of the wicked leads them astray" (Proverbs 12:26).

Additionally, I love the guidelines that writer and artist Jackie Hill Perry gives for what type of people these close friends should be like. She advised recently on Twitter, "Get friends that make: (1) Sin look bad, (2) God look big, (3) Grace look tangible, and (4) The Gospel look true."[6]

Your Sounding Board of Sisters

If you don't already have one, start praying now about setting up a support system of two or three other wives who will act as your covenant friends, pledging to honestly share and eagerly pray for each other's marriages, not just during a six-week Bible study but for the long haul. Then connect regularly to honestly share and pray for each other. I didn't say to husband-bash or even to vent. If you spend time with other wives complaining about your husbands and giving each other just "Oh, you poor baby, he's being a jerk" feedback, it won't help your marriage improve.

Share openly. Be each other's sounding board. Be willing to allow them to speak tough truths to you, letting you know if they think you said or did something you should apologize for. In fact, find friends who will be brave enough to take your husband's side in a dispute if they feel he is right! I often tease two of my closest covenant friends, saying that if Todd and I make it to our fiftieth anniversary, I'm sending them thank-you notes because they are such friends to me.

If you can't physically meet together due to proximity, there are other ways you can connect. My safety-net group of friends connects through our phones, often texting Scriptures to each other. Sometimes we give a quick prayer request. If the prayer request is a little more involved, we may send a group email or use the Voxer app to leave a voice communication. (Voxer is like a walkie-talkie that can be listened to in real time or the messages can be retrieved later when you want to hear them.) We also try to schedule a conference call once a month where we can take turns sharing and then both listen to and give feedback. We close the time together by praying for each other, and then we get back to our families and lives.

Your Couples Community

Is there at least one other Christian couple you can spend time with, sharing not only your struggles but your joys? Being in community can make the difference between atrophy and improvement in your marriage. The wonderful flip side of such relationships is that the other couple is not just helping you; you are getting to encourage them as well. This forces you to not be so self-focused. Also, you'll often find that in urging another couple to keep showing up and keep granting grace, you are inspired to keep doing the same things yourself.

There's no magical formula as to how—and how often—you should connect with this couple (or even with a few couples). You may want to start a weekly Bible study. Or you could go out to dinner once a month. My friend Marcia, to whom this book is dedicated, is married to my husband's friend Phil. Our get-togethers are very informal. Sometimes we just spend time munching on popcorn and sitting in one of our living rooms processing life together. Other dear married friends of ours enjoy nostalgic outdoor concerts, just like we do. Together, we throw down an old blanket on the hillside and listen to a band play some oldies. Then we go out for appetizers and have a long heart-to-heart with each other. We often stay out until the wee hours of the morning until the restaurant closes for the night.

Pray that God will direct you to another couple you can hang out with regularly. Now, you may not want to just walk up to them and say, "Hey, wanna get together every so often to spill our guts?" Start with getting to know them informally, spending time doing an activity like bowling, miniature golf, or going out for a movie and supper. This way, you can see if you all hit it off and might make good accountability partners for each other.

Your Crucial Confidante

Finally comes your locked box, as I like to call it. Your crucial confidante. That one friend with whom you can share all the details—with your husband's blessing, of course—and process and pray earnestly. In the Bible, we read, "Two are better than one, because they have a good return for their labor: If either of them falls down, one can help the other up. But pity anyone who falls and has no one to help them up" (Ecclesiastes 4:9–10).

You need a trustworthy, I've-got-your-back friend who will help you up when you fall. Make sure it's a woman who has your best interests at heart and who is a strong believer, someone who won't just give her opinion but will share advice that is in line with God's Word. It's essential that this person is willing to say the hard things—like my friend Mary did when she told me I needed to stop expecting Todd to do everything my way. Proverbs 27:6 tells us that wounds from a friend are trustworthy. In other words, a friend will say something that may sting only because they want your marriage to improve.

Keep this friend in your "Favorites" tab on your phone. Don't wear out your welcome, of course, contacting her every single time your husband looks sideways at you, but make sure each of you feels the freedom to make contact for emergency prayer.

Commit to praying daily for one another. Listen attentively. Answer cautiously and prayerfully. Act as a spotter should you see her begin to wobble. Reach up and steady her so she doesn't come crashing down.

SISTER KEEPING

A few days ago, my elderly neighbor called me. At first, she just seemed like she wanted to chat a bit about the weather and our son's new Alaskan Malamute puppy Aspen, whom she'd seen running around our side yard. Then she told me the real reason for her call. "Oh, Karen, it's just *so good* to hear your voice. I haven't seen you outside lately—or your car come and go out of the garage—and so I was afraid maybe something was wrong. Is everything okay with you and Todd?"

Now, some people in my shoes might have been offended that she would ask whether my husband and I were doing okay. But I thought it was more than neighborly of her—it was downright sweet and touching. She's not the gossipy, gadabout sort. I knew she was generally concerned for us.

I myself have had times when I stopped seeing either a husband or wife around the neighborhood. Or when one half of a couple no longer came to church. And in a few cases, a family that would never fail to send out a Christmas card with an update letter and family picture inside didn't do so one year. Soon after all these occurrences, I found out the couple was splitting up.

Maybe more of us need to be nosy—in a neighborly sort of way.

We may also need to have some skin in the game, contributing money for another couple to attend counseling or go to a marriage conference. Or maybe we could put in time by watching our friends' kids while they go on a much-needed date to talk. Don't be afraid to get all up in the mess of another friend's life—letting them return the favor. True friendship costs us, but it also pays fabulous returns.

Author Stephen Covey once suggested, "Accountability breeds *response-ability*."[7] When we have someone keeping us accountable, we acquire an ability to respond to life properly.

So, in a way we are our sister's keeper—our steadfast friendship can help keep her showing up in her marriage, glorifying God as she does.

Do all you can to set yourself up for success in your relationship with your husband.

Don't let your mind produce a terrifying trailer when you survey the scenes of your marriage. Reframe the bad times, thanking Jesus for how they drive you closer to him.

Notice and appreciate even the smallest of blessings, thanking God daily for their constant presence in our life.

Find friends and other couples who can catch you when you fall—and better yet, who will speak up if they see you start to wobble.

When you experience authentic Christian community, you will be following what the Bible encourages us to do: "Let us consider how we may spur one another on toward love and good deeds, not giving up meeting together, as some are in the habit of doing, but encouraging one another—and all the more as you see the Day approaching" (Hebrews 10:24–25).

The time of Jesus' return grows closer with each passing day. Encourage one another. Spur each other on. Don't be afraid to give—and receive—an occasional (and needed!) kick in the pants.

Don't just keep showing up for your husband. Keep doing it for your covenant friends as well.

NINE

Never Stop Starting Over

♥

Tomorrow is a new day with no mistakes in it yet.
ANNE OF GREEN GABLES

The steadfast love of the LORD never ceases;
his mercies never come to an end; they are new
every morning; great is your faithfulness.
LAMENTATIONS 3:22–23 ESV

My home office is not an upscale workstation. The walls are decorated with an eclectic collection of antique plates of varied shapes and sizes, all in the color scheme of aqua, pink, and white. I gathered them from area garage and estate sales over the years, none costing more than a buck. My Craigslist desk sports a retro pink phone, complete with a curly cord—a leftover from my daughter's days as a teenager. Snapshots of close relatives smile at me as I write, a visual reminder for me to pray for them before I start my day. A large, smooth rock from the bottom of Duck Lake serves as a handy paperweight for bills, letters, and the like, and was purchased from my great-step-nephew's beachside road stand.

However, the most cherished element of my cozy cubicle is a

weathered wooden sign. I glance at it each morning when I turn on the light, my steaming mug of coffee in hand. It watches over me as I start flipping things open—first my Bible to connect with Jesus and then my laptop to begin my workday. It's also the last item that catches my eye before leaving my office in the late afternoon to walk to the kitchen to start supper simmering on the stove.

This sign has saved me headaches. And heartache. It has adjusted my attitude when it was starting to grow grouchy and caused my just-about-to-unload lips to keep tightly closed. Spying it standing there silently has prompted me to wipe the tears from my eyes and keep loving Todd—despite what he'd just done and how it made me feel. What are these magic words strategically stenciled on this aging sign? It reads:

JUNE 21, 1986
221 GUESTS

When Todd and I recited our wedding vows, we didn't do so holding hands and gazing into each other's eyes with no one else around. We also spoke them before the 221 family members and friends who showed up that early summer day. And—most importantly—they were also pronounced in the presence of God.

Whenever thoughts like, *Why in the world did I ever marry this guy? I'm outta here!* tear through my brain, canceling out any feelings of affection and turning up the heat on my nearly boiling blood . . . I stop.

I reread the sign. I recall that June afternoon and decide that—even though I'm totally ticked off at my man—I will keep my word. The word I gave in front of those people and the vows I gave before the Lord.

Who knew an old piece of wood could possess such spiritual sway?

WHAT IS WRONG WITH THE WORLD (THAT IS A STATEMENT, NOT A QUESTION!)

I hopped on my Twitter account last week to briefly catch up on any news I had missed over the previous two days. I'd been away from home at a bed-and-breakfast and delightfully unplugged from my phone. When I clicked on the link for trending topics, I started shaking—and also scratching—my head as I read both some bizarre and some concerning happenings. As I toggled between "Teens eating laundry pods" and "Regime unleashes chemical attack" I wondered out loud, "What in the world is wrong with people?"

This question is effortlessly—and often—posed when we are looking at others. We may see peculiar behavior. We may witness the cruel actions of one human toward another. Closer to home, we look at the people with whom we share a house, an office, or a street, and sometimes they too say or do something that makes us contemplate, *What in the world is wrong with you people?*

Years ago, a British newspaper was said to have posed a question in one of its issues. It invited readers to answer this query: "What is wrong with the world?" Many people undoubtedly responded with essays espousing all of the ills plaguing society. But one journalist, G. K. Chesterton, sent perhaps one of the shortest essays on this topic ever written. He succinctly replied, "Dear Sir, I am. Yours sincerely, G. K. Chesterton."[1]

His response was not only brief but insightful, for it perfectly sums up the whole reason for the gospel, its refreshing and redemptive message ever unchanged.

The fifth chapter of Romans lays out this whole "What in the world is wrong?" dilemma. The problem? Our sin. Sin entered the world through one man—Adam. This sin led to death—not just for our ancestor Adam, but it had a ripple effect of mortality on all of us who would ever set foot on this earth: "Sin entered the world through one man, and death through sin, and in this way death came to all people, *because all sinned*" (Romans 5:12, emphasis mine).

See those three words—*because all sinned*? There has never been a person born who was without sin, except for Jesus himself when he took on human flesh (John 1:14; Philippians 2:7).

Sin separates us from God and prevents us from spending eternity with him in heaven someday. Sin is serious business. A penalty must be paid for it. And no amount of good behavior on our part can ever allow us to bypass this penalty, to skirt around the sin or hide it somehow and gain entrance into heaven nonetheless.

Thankfully, God sent his Son to pay the price and take our place: "You see, at just the right time, when we were still powerless, Christ died for the ungodly. Very rarely will anyone die for a righteous person, though for a good person someone might possibly dare to die. But God demonstrates his own love for us in this: While we were still sinners, Christ died for us" (Romans 5:6–8).

Hallelujah and amen. But wait—not so fast. Before we break out in our happy dance, there is more to this glorious story.

When we place our trust in the finished work of Jesus on the cross to cancel our debt of sin, it is as if he stands in front of us when we face judgment. God looks at sinful us and instead sees sinless Jesus. However, in your remaining days on earth, you are still going to sin at times.

So is your spouse.

And your kids.

And that sweet, soft-spoken woman who never misses church, her hand-lettered and colorfully illustrated Bible open on her lap each week.

Yes. Her too.

We *all* still sin.

What happens in marriage is that we often place our spouse's sin under a magnifying glass, enlarging it and identifying it as the crux of our conflict. But to find our own sin—well, we'd need a microscope. Oh sure, we admit that it's there, but we also argue how teeny-tiny it is.

It's a snap to spot and highlight wrong behavior in our mate. Continually doing so—to the neglect of acknowledging our own sinful behavior—keeps the merry-go-round of conflict spinning nearly out of control.

Only when we echo the words of Mr. Chesterton will we ever see any progress. Friends, *we* are what is wrong with the world—our sin is the setback from which all that is ugly and awful emerges.

> *The first fifty years of marriage are always the hardest.*
>
> *Anonymous*

We'll acknowledge that sin festers in the conspiring mind of the leader of an evil regime. We readily recognize that it dwells in the callused heart of the cold-blooded school shooter. We observe it held tightly in the clenched fist of the domestic abuser. We spot it in a heartbeat in the actions of those who rape, torment, taunt, discriminate, or destroy.

We just politely ignore it in ourselves.

It's time we all learned to mind our own sin.

I don't mean we turn a blind eye or deaf ears to the cries of those affected by the sin of others. We fight for the abused, the marginalized, the oppressed. We do what we can to combat the effects of sin in the world. But first? We turn our eyes and ears toward our own hearts, dealing promptly and properly with our own sin—especially in our marriage.

Remember, it all comes down to you and Jesus. No guarantees

promised about your spouse's behavior, no assurance that you'll live ever-so-happily after all.

You can only commit to mind your own sin—own up to it, repent of it, ask forgiveness for it, and then turn in the opposite direction and keep moving on. This is what positions us for growth spiritually.

GROWING TOGETHER IN CHANGE

If your husband is also a believer who wants to follow God's words, your marriage can be the place where God's grace abounds and his love is lived out. (If he's not, please keep reading. There are hope-filled stories and words in the rest of the chapter. And may I suggest—if you haven't already done so—that you read the sidebar on page 166 titled "When You're Not Spiritually in Sync.") You can learn to not only expect but accept the changes and growth that happen in your spouse, if you are both intent to never stop maturing in your individual walks with the Lord—and in turn in your relationship with each other.

My friend Bailey and I were chatting about marriage the other day. She and her husband, Jacob, married millennials, began dating as ninth graders more than a decade ago. They've watched each other grow up right before their eyes and have witnessed many changes in each other.

Bailey uttered some very wise words: "One thing will be true throughout our lives: we will continue to change and be different. I hear people say they left their spouse because they changed. When people say that, I'm shocked. Didn't they know that was one of the things they were signing up for—change? Life experiences are constantly going to change things about us. It's important to make sure that God is the one changing us, and not the world. We must both individually sit before God and spend time with him. It never fails that if I go to the Lord, he will quickly point out the areas where I'm weak and need him. It's my job to listen and allow him to refine me rather than to try to change my husband."

It frustrates me greatly to not be able to make my husband change. But I can take Bailey's advice and go to God with my own areas of weakness and leave the refining of my husband up to God. He will be faithful to change me for the good, using my marriage in the process. Don't resist change, clutching tightly and refusing to let go. Pry your hands off the control knob of life. Rivet your eyes on Jesus. Stand back and watch him work in both of your lives.

We sometimes hesitate when we think we have to give up something to follow Jesus. We don't realize we will acquire something even better when we do.

WHEN HOPELESSNESS PRESSES IN

I've not only witnessed the way God has used Todd to mold and shape my heart and grow me up in the faith, but I've also seen this happen with many of my friends—some of whom have serious stories. A few have agreed to let me share their struggles with you. If you feel hopeless in your marriage, I hope their stories will show you that you're not alone.

In life, sometimes we choose our challenges, and other times, our challenges choose us. Here are three friends of mine whose challenges chose them. I've watched them respond by living out the gospel, even when the days were dark.

Kris and Nicki

Nineteen-year-old Nicki found herself standing at an altar, pregnant by a man she'd only been dating for a few months and barely even knew. In six weeks' time, she went from standing in the bathroom staring in shock at a pregnancy test to standing before the preacher, saying, "I do." A man from the church who gave Nicki and her fiancé, Kris, some hurried-up marital counseling before the wedding told them they had every odd against them and their marriage probably wouldn't make it.

For the first five or so years, Nicki says she regularly told her husband in anger, "I don't want to be married to you—at all." She had been deeply wounded by people in her life and was trying desperately to have her husband fill a deep void inside her. When he couldn't, she lashed out. Kris himself had some personal struggles that only added more layers of difficulty onto their relationship. Facing their troubles wasn't at all easy, but one day they decided that at least they wanted to try.

They went to counseling. They kept showing up. More and more, Nicki found herself feeling grateful that she was Kris's wife. She was deeply remorseful for all the times over the years that she'd told him she didn't want to be married to him.

Nicki says she had unconsciously adopted a template for what a godly man looked like, and Kris just didn't fit it. But she now sees that the template was legalistic and unattainable. It only left her feeling disappointed. "Now I see what real commitment is. It's the man who stayed when there was nothing good in our marriage. The man who stayed when there wasn't any money. The man who stays by your side when your mom is dying. That is a good man."

She said today her marriage is not at all what you'd call easy, but they keep staying the course, ready to get help when they need it. "It's true that death and life are in the power of the tongue. I was speaking death over my marriage by telling Kris I hated being his wife," she said. "Now I see the beautiful story that God has written in the lives of two nineteen-year-old, super-messed-up kids. We kept working on our marriage and kept believing that God could change our hearts, and he did."

Jeff and Melissa

Melissa and Jeff's marriage started out healthy and relatively uneventful twenty-eight years ago. However, as four kids came along, accompanied by mounting financial and relational strain, stress began to take its toll on their marriage. "There wasn't a big blowup, but more like a slow leaking of love," Melissa recalls. "We eventually grew apart and grew bitter."

About twelve years ago, they were sleeping in separate rooms, going through the motions, and harboring ever greater grudges toward each other. Then came the day Melissa points to as the turning point. "We finally talked. I was certain at this point that our marriage was not going to make it. I looked at Jeff and asked him one question: 'Is there any hope for us?' I will never forget his response. He looked at me and said, 'One ounce.'"

I know that doesn't sound very hopeful, but Melissa said, "I thought, *I am taking that one ounce and running to Jesus.*" She figured if Jesus could do miracles like feeding five thousand people with a few loaves and a couple of fish, he could take that one tiny ounce of hope and make her marriage not only last but become strong.

She focused on her own spiritual growth. She became convicted that she needed to not be a pushy wife. While they were both Christians, Jeff wasn't really interested in spiritual things. He thought of Melissa's going to church and Bible studies as her hobby. But slowly, over time, God began to change Jeff just as he was changing his wife. Jeff bought Melissa a little figurine of a girl holding a tiny balloon. Inside it was one word—*hope.*

After counseling and prayer, honesty and forgiveness, and years of continuing to show up and work on their relationship, they are still together and ever grateful. "We laughed just last night, as we ate pizza and watched TV together, at what a boring marriage we have." She added, "But who cares? We're still together. God took that hope and grew it. Jesus saved our marriage." Today both Jeff and Melissa serve in their local church and are a testimony to the way Jesus changes everything—if we will only let him.

Chris and Cindy

Cindy was unpacking boxes one afternoon, having just moved to a new city with her husband, Chris, and their three-year-old son. She was joyful and looking forward to the future. Then, in the course of about sixty seconds, her life came crashing down all around her when her husband—a pastor—told her they needed to talk.

Chris made a startling confession. He had been viewing pornography and meeting women online. And over the course of the previous two and a half years, he had been unfaithful to Cindy with several of them. Then came even more shocking information. One of the women, with whom he had been multiple times, was now pregnant with his child.

Cindy recalls, "In addition to the immediate onset of writhing pain, I began to imagine life as a single mom to our three-year-old little boy. I went straight into the pit of despair. I just didn't want to be alive anymore. It was that bad. I wasn't going to take my life, but it would have been okay if somebody else had."

As they talked, and she asked questions, Chris sobbed out his answers. Cindy realized that her husband's heart was sincerely broken and that he was truly sorry for his actions. Still, with biblical grounds for divorce and a marriage and ministry now both wrecked, Cindy had to decide if she would leave her husband. How could she ever find the strength to stay in the marriage, forgive the infidelity, and rebuild what was now in shambles?

It was then that God spoke to her through a very unlikely minor prophet named Habakkuk. In her Bible she read, "For the revelation awaits an appointed time; it speaks of the end and will not prove false. Though it linger, wait for it; it will certainly come and will not delay" (Habakkuk 2:3).

Cindy says, "That verse was the very word I needed from God, and it was confirmed to me by two people on the same day. I heard God whisper this hope to my heart: 'My child, I know you don't understand what I am asking of you. You don't think anything good can come from this. But I need you to trust me. And one day, you will see me work all of this for your good and my glory.'"

And so—she chose to stay.

Chris resigned from his position at church and took a job at a hardware store. They worked on rebuilding their marriage. A few years later, Cindy gave birth to another son. And the other woman—whom Cindy eventually met—had Chris's baby, also a son. Today, Chris is back on staff at church. Their marriage is intact, healthy, and a picture of God's redemption. His son from the affair stays with Cindy and Chris on holidays and in the summer. He hangs out with his half-brothers and is a welcomed and loved part of the family.

It has no doubt been painful. Cindy says of the journey to healing, "I trusted God when it felt normal and when it felt abnormal. Basically, I never gave up—through the pain, through the devastation, through the turmoil. Most of all, I learned that had I never needed comfort, I would not have known my Comforter."

Cindy had biblical grounds for divorcing her husband. I would not fault someone in her shoes at all for doing so. I would support them any way I could. However, part of her decision to stay came when a wise, older man looked her in the eyes and said, "I would respect you if you felt that you needed to remove yourself from your marriage. What you've endured is very hard. But you are not a fool to stay and be a part of the redemptive work in a man's life."[2]

And we are not fools if we hold fast to God when our marriages also encounter trials—however temporary and tiny or earth-shattering and severe. When the world screams, "Walk away!" Jesus often whispers, "Trust me. I will give you the strength to stay."

BECAUSE YOU SAY SO

Weddings today have become a grandstand of sorts. The average wedding in America now costs more than $35,000.[3] Of course, this can vary by zip code. For fun, I looked up the zip code where my daughter now lives, and for the size wedding Todd and I had with those 221 guests, the total spent today on a wedding can be upward of $65,000![4] Gulp. Our entire celebration—including the dress, flowers, decorations, and a tasty cold buffet of home-made sandwiches and salads—rang up at right around $1,200. (Which was actually $200 over the budget my parents gave me, so I chipped in the extra myself!)

If it isn't a financially impressive event, pressure exists to make sure the wedding day is Pinterest-perfect, with everything stenciled, stitched up, hot glued, and showcased in a DIY contest of creativity.

We also love to observe over-the-top nuptials unfold on our television screens. The extravagant marriage of reality star Kim Kardashian and NBA player Kris Humphries in August 2011 cost a reported 10 million dollars and was viewed by more than

4 million people over the two nights the whole grand affair was aired on October 9 and 10 of that year. Just three weeks later, on Halloween, the new bride filed for divorce—just seventy-two days into their marriage, citing as her reason "irreconcilable differences."

Many argue that the marriage was all for show anyway—as in the literal reality show *Keeping Up with the Kardashians* that drew so many gawkers when it aired. Whatever the case, the ins and outs of their courtship, marriage, and subsequent divorce were watched by curious people all over the globe.

Hanging in there in marriage doesn't draw quite as big a crowd.

If you commit to mind your own sin, go to God with your cares and concerns, and do the hard behind-the-scenes work of continuing to show up in your marriage, there will be no great applause. I hope your safety-net circle of friends will cheer you on as you make progress, encouraging you to model Jesus in your interactions with your husband. But most usually, you will find yourself alone—just you and the Lord. He may be the only one to witness your marital tenacity.

Recently I took a train to Chicago to spend a few days with a new client, helping her craft a message to give when she speaks. After making a scheduled stop to pick up more passengers, the train pulled out of the depot, slowly meandering through the countryside of southwest Michigan. Before it got up to full speed, we came to a wide space of fields where mostly brown and beige weeds and overgrown briars grew as far as the eye could see. However, up ahead in the distance, my eye caught a sudden splash of brilliant lavender that stood in stark contrast to the bland, unbecoming foliage.

As the train traveled on, this patch of purple came more clearly into view. There in the landscape stood the biggest and most gorgeous lilac bush I have ever spied in my life, the blooms so enormous I thought they might topple the bush right over. I thought to myself what a shame it was that this magnificent spectacle of nature was situated way out there in the boondocks where hardly anyone could see it.

But you know what? The remote location of that breathtaking bush does not detract from its splendor. It matters not that it draws few onlookers. It is still a stunning display of growth and life. Not having an audience does not make it any less lovely.

Your marriage is that bush.

As you grow and blossom, showing up and showing Jesus, most likely you won't gather a large audience.

Grow and blossom anyway.

The gospel of Luke records an account of Jesus and Peter—and also Peter's fellow fishermen, James and John. As was often the case, a crowd of people was nearby. Let's read through the story:

> One day as Jesus was standing by the Lake of Gennesaret, the people were crowding around him and listening to the word of God. He saw at the water's edge two boats, left there by the fishermen, who were washing their nets. He got into one of the boats, the one belonging to Simon, and asked him to put out a little from shore. Then he sat down and taught the people from the boat.
>
> When he had finished speaking, he said to Simon, "Put out into deep water, and let down the nets for a catch."
>
> Simon answered, "Master, we've worked hard all night and haven't caught anything. But because you say so, I will let down the nets."
>
> When they had done so, they caught such a large number of fish that their nets began to break. So they signaled

their partners in the other boat to come and help them, and they came and filled both boats so full that they began to sink.

When Simon Peter saw this, he fell at Jesus' knees and said, "Go away from me, Lord; I am a sinful man!" For he and all his companions were astonished at the catch of fish they had taken, and so were James and John, the sons of Zebedee, Simon's partners.

Then Jesus said to Simon, "Don't be afraid; from now on you will fish for people." So they pulled their boats up on shore, left everything and followed him.

Luke 5:1–11

What was the key to this miraculous snagging of fish?

Verse 5: "But because you say so, I will let down the nets."

Peter and his buddies had been fishing all night—doing things their usual way—to no avail. But when Jesus showed up, it changed everything.

Even though the rough-and-tumble fishermen didn't understand, they did what the Lord told them to do. When Peter witnessed the power of Jesus by the change in his circumstances, he fell at his feet, recognizing his sin in stark contrast to the sinless Savior who stood before him. But Jesus didn't allow him to stay stuck in his sin. He calmed his fears, lifted his spirits, and gave him a new, more eternity-minded assignment.

From now on you will fish for people.

Peter and his friends abandoned their normal; they left everything behind and followed Jesus.

Fishing for people means spreading the gospel—both with our words and by our actions. There is no better place to display the gospel than smack-dab in the center of your marriage.

Show the gospel to your husband. Your kids. Others in your

life who may also be watching. Stop doing things the same old—dare I say normal?—way.

Listen to Jesus, and then cast your net. Why?

Because he says so.

JUST DO IT—FOR JESUS

My friend Macey is a middle school counselor in an economically depressed school district in Georgia. In her building, several students are not only in financial trouble, but also often in trouble with the administration. Some are even in trouble with the law.

Macey is an incredible academic professional who views her secular vocation as a sacred ministry. She goes far beyond her required duties of punching in, seeing students, and putting in hours filing paperwork and administering assessment tests. She throws herself into her occupation enthusiastically, making a concerted effort to develop respectful and loving relationships with her kids. She does this with even the most difficult students, recognizing many of them are acting out due to horrible situations outside of school.

Recently, she told me about one such child who was in trouble with the administration. He was given the chance to remain in school after an incident, as long as he agreed to go to in-school suspension and take his discipline. This included writing the rules of in-school suspension out by hand. He was not cooperating with the suspension assignment and refused to write out the rules. That is, until Miss Macey showed up.

She knew of this student's struggles. She had prayed for him often. She realized students in his situation had the potential to get volatile and blow up, also blowing any chances of staying in school because they would then be expelled.

When she got in the room, she tried an idea she believed

might work. She firmly but lovingly looked at this troubled boy and assured him she totally understood that writing sentences was a drag. However, she had a trick up her sleeve—one that could save him heartache and prevent him from being kicked out.

"Look, I know you don't want to do this. Writing out rules is no fun. But—tell you what—will you do something? Will you please just do it for me?"

He thought about it for a few seconds. Soon his pencil was making its way across the paper. He had no desire to write out rules, which caused his hand to become all cramped up. But he did it for Miss Macey—the person who had taken the time to notice his situation and love him despite his behavior.

Marriage is hard work. Doing it right sometimes cramps our style. It hurts. And some days, we just don't feel like doing it.

If you want to give up—or stay married physically but become emotionally divorced and distant—if you want to stop trying to live in harmony with that man who aggravates and infuriates you so; if everything in you longs to stop showing up and just walk away and be done with it . . .

Listen to Jesus. The one who sees your situation and takes note of your struggles, the one who, despite your own bad behavior, loves you regardless. He is lovingly looking you in the eyes today and saying, "Look, I know you don't want to do this. But—tell you what—will you do something? Will you please just do it for me?"

HALF THE BATTLE

Our friends Duane and Kate hopped into the back seat of our Buick as we headed north on US 127 to attend an outdoor concert. That evening, we sat on our plaid blankets and soaked in the late-evening summer sun while listening to Don Henley from the legendary group the Eagles crank out some of our favorite hits from back in the day. After the performance, we planned to grab a bite to eat and spend time talking late into the night, catching up and encouraging each other in the midst of whatever problems and obstacles we were facing. (With eleven kids between us, we're never lacking in the "problems and obstacles" department!)

I love our friendship with this couple. We've known Duane for more than twenty-five years, and his children and ours are like siblings. We met Kate a decade ago when they first began dating. They are both in their second marriage, their first marriages each having ended at the request of their former spouses. Their beautiful blended family includes eight children, two sons-in-law and two daughters-in-law, and three grandkids—with one more grandbaby on the way.

The manner in which each of them handled their unwanted divorce spoke volumes to those who were watching. They held on to the hope that is ours in Christ, even when circumstances were bleak. When they were left single, they took their brokenness to God and trusted him with their futures.

Today, the priority they put on making God the center of their marriage inspires and encourages Todd and me so much. Plus, they are loads of fun! They are the reverse of Todd and me—with Kate having Todd's laid-back personality and Duane and I always chatting—rarely stopping long enough to take a breath. We carve out time with them whenever we can and help each other get life done, putting on parties, graduations, and such. (Just one more high school graduation to go, and then our roasters can rest!)

At the end of the concert, after Duane and I—both huge Eagles fans—had sung every song at the top of our lungs while our spouses looked on and politely smiled, Don Henley took to the microphone one last time to thank the crowd for spending the nostalgic evening with him.

"Thank you so much for showing up. Keep showing up. After all, isn't that half the battle?"

It *is* half the battle. And thankfully, the *whole* battle belongs to the Lord.

It is God's business to fight for us. Our assignment is to keep reporting for duty—ready to learn and love, knowing "we can handle some resistance if our love is a strong one." (← See what I did right there, fellow Eagles fans?)

Are you ready to go the distance, focusing on your own behavior instead of constantly pointing out the flaws of your spouse? (*Ahem . . .* another self-sermon.)

Will you place a high value on learning to deal with conflict in a healthy way, refusing to allow emotional baggage, unmet expectations, and incorrect perceptions to muddy the marital waters?

Will you reframe romance, finding the magic in the mundane and trying hard to speak your spouse's love language?

Will you mind your own sin, taking it to Jesus, who will forgive us when we confess and turn away from it?

Will you persevere, doing it even though the only one who sees the budding of your spiritual growth is the Lord himself?

Don't expect your spouse to behave. Oh, sometimes he will. Other times he will get on your very last nerve—driving you completely crazy and right up the nearest wall. At those times, remember that God forgives our own sins, sparing us the punishment we so rightly deserve.

If he can do that—and he already did—then I certainly can choose to forgive my spouse.

So can you.

Let Ephesians 4:32 serve as our earnest aim and our constant reminder: "Be kind and compassionate to one another, forgiving each other, just as in Christ God forgave you."

We forgive today . . . and tomorrow . . . and the next day . . . *because God already forgave us.*

Never stop starting over.

Do it now.

Do it daily.

Do it just for Jesus.

Just keep showing up.

ACKNOWLEDGMENTS

To my Proverbs 31 Ministries brothers (yes, we have three men on staff!) and sisters: I simply love serving Jesus alongside each of you. What an immense honor!

To our Proverbs 31 Ministries president, Lysa TerKeurst: you are the best boss-friend a person could ever ask for. And yes, I just coined a new word. #bossfriendsarethebomb

To my publishing manager, Meredith Brock: what a gift you are to my all-over-the-map ideas, bringing them into a strategic focus! I can't imagine doing ministry without you.

To my HarperCollins Christian family—vice president of marketing Tom Dean, marketing associate Bridgette Brooks, senior editor Greg Clouse, Zondervan vice president and publisher David Morris, and especially associate publisher and executive editor Sandy Vander Zicht, who has been with me for all of my first six books at Zondervan and who, sadly, will be retired by the time this book goes into print (somebody grab me a hankie!): it takes more than a village to publish a book—it takes a small country. Thank you all for being my fellow countrymen (and women!).

To my editor Lori Vanden Bosch: thank you for your expert editing, tweaking, and polishing of my rough manuscript. Most of all, thank you for your genuine encouragement of my writing ministry.

To my *Behind-the-Scenes Queens* Facebook community: bless you girls (and one guy—my husband!) for being willing at a moment's notice to pray, process, and give feedback on my ideas, covers, titles, and such. Y'all are the best!

To my fabulous virtual assistant and even fabulous-er friend, Kim Stewart: your insight, ideas, social-media savvy, and hard work are appreciated more than you will ever know. I mean, like, it would take me three or four whole fifteen-minute Voxers to convey my heartfelt sentiments about how much I love working with you! You are so speedy and efficient that I still wonder if there are actually two of you.

To my now fully grown little people Kenna, Mitchell, and Spencer: being your mom is the third greatest privilege of my life, only trumped by being your dad's girlfriend and serving Jesus. There are no other people Dad and I would rather spend alone time with—yes, even when we take breathtakingly adventurous cross-country trips, pausing our sightseeing just long enough to lodge in exceedingly cheap hotel rooms, usually one of the chains with a number in the title. #familybondingintheboondocks

To my college sweetheart-turned-husband Todd: let's never stop starting over. I love Jesus more than you. I know you love him more than me too. Let's just keep it that way. This plan has worked well for thirty-two years, so why stop now? I love you and I like you.

To my Lord and Savior, Jesus Christ: for dying on the cross for my sins and then teaching me daily to die to myself. Indescribable.

Verses for When It's You Versus Him

Ephesians 4:32: "Be kind and compassionate
to one another, forgiving each other,
just as in Christ God forgave you."

1 Peter 4:8: "Above all, love each other deeply,
because love covers over a multitude of sins."

Romans 12:10: "Be devoted to one another in
love. Honor one another above yourselves."

Ephesians 4:2-3: "Be completely humble and
gentle; be patient, bearing with one another
in love. Make every effort to keep the unity
of the Spirit through the bond of peace."

Luke 6:31: "Do to others as you
would have them do to you."

REALITY CHECK REMINDERS

Following are some quotes from the book that may be helpful for you to keep before you. Simply photocopy them on card stock, cut them out, and let them serve as visual reminders for you to keep showing up and keep showing Jesus in your relationship with your husband.

> **Marriage is hard and it's not about me.**

> **Your marriage is a message, and people are watching you preach.**

> **Will you dare to love, serve, and sacrifice, doing it only for an audience of One?**

Fight fair and
behave like Jesus.

Don't hang up on your marriage.
Hang in there instead.

He's not just my husband.
He is also my brother in Christ.

My husband is my husband.
He is not my God.

Pick love when you'd
rather pick a fight.

Keep looking for the magic
in the midst of the mundane.

Every marriage is a unique
blend of awesome and awful.

Questions for Finding Your Ministry as a Couple

1. Are there any areas in life where you feel you already have a ministry together? If so, what are they?

2. List any people or groups of people you know in your church or community who are in pain—physically, emotionally, relationally, or financially. Then look back over what you wrote and try to think of at least one way you can help each person or group you mentioned.

3. When you think of the concept of "finding your old self," what ideas for ministry come to mind?

4. Each of you list three to five interests you have that could lead you to a ministry. Then list some ways this passion or hobby might be used to help others (for example, you love to work in the yard, mowing the lawn or weeding your flower

beds—perhaps you could have a summertime ministry doing this for an elderly couple at church who can still live alone in their home but can no longer perform outdoor maintenance).

5. Could any of the areas you listed above be something the two of you could do together? If so, which ones and how could both of you be a part?

6. In what ways could you use your home for ministry?

7. How might you use any items you own for ministry—your car, your washer and dryer, your lawn mower, or any tools you own?

8. If you have children, how could you incorporate them into one of the possible ministries you have mentioned?

9. What is one action step you can take to make a trial run at one of the ideas you've discussed above? Put a reminder on your phone or in your calendar app to revisit this, and make sure you follow through on it.

NOTES

Chapter 1: Where Does a Wife Go to Resign?

1. Quoted in Cynthia Crossen, "A Not-So-Perfect Union," *Wall Street Journal*, June 27, 2008, www.wsj.com/articles/SB1214425 01390504433.

Chapter 2: Embracing Your Sandpaper Spouse

1. Paul David Tripp, *What Did You Expect? Redeeming the Realities of Marriage* (Wheaton, IL: Crossway, 2010), 67.

2. Quoted in Ellen Baumler, *Montana Moments: History on the Go* (Helena: Montana Historical Society Press, 2010), 90.

3. Chuck Swindoll, "Charles R. Swindoll Papers," Archives, Dallas Theological Seminary, in *An Uncommon Union: Dallas Theological Seminary and American Evangelism*, ed. John D. Hannah (Grand Rapids: Zondervan, 2009), 225.

4. Quoted in Donald J. Davidson, *The Wisdom of Theodore Roosevelt* (New York: Citadel, 2003), 90–91.

5. See Alexandra Witze, "Astronaut Twin Study Hints at Stress of Space Travel," January 26, 2017, www.nature.com/news/astronaut-twin-study-hints-at-stress-of-space-travel-1.21380; see update, Elizabeth Howell, "Astronaut Scott Kelly and His Twin Brother Are Still Identical, NASA Says," March 16, 2018,

www.space.com/40007-astronauts-scott-mark-kelly-still
-identical.html.

Chapter 4: Duel or Duet? Your Choice

1. Scott Sauls, Twitter post, 11:15 a.m., June 6, 2018, https://twitter
   .com/scottsauls/status/1004436562078248960.
2. Quoted in Robby Brumberg, "The Enduring Wit and Warmth of
   Billy Graham," Ragan.com, February 22, 2018, www.ragan.com/
   the-enduring-wit-and-warmth-of-billy-graham.
3. C. S. Lewis, *Mere Christianity* (1952; repr., San Francisco:
   HarperOne, 2001), 115.

Chapter 5: You've Lost That Lovin' Feelin'

1. Orison Swett Marden, *How to Get What You Want* (New York:
   Crowell, 1917), 74.
2. Cited in "Madonna on Marriage, from 'The Sunday Times,'"
   November 7, 2005, www.24-7prayer.com/blog/456/madonna-on
   -marriage-from-the-sunday-times.
3. Becky Thompson, *Love Unending: Rediscovering Your Marriage
   in the Midst of Motherhood* (Colorado Springs: WaterBrook,
   2017).

Chapter 6: Finding Magic in the Mundane

1. Gary Chapman, *The Five Love Languages: The Secret to Love
   That Lasts* (1992; repr., Chicago: Northfield, 2015).
2. Jackie Hill Perry, Twitter post, 7:22 a.m., March 1, 2018, https://
   twitter.com/jackiehillperry/status/969231529997160448.

Chapter 7: The Mission of Your Marriage

1. Quoted in Kristy Robinson Horine, "The Couple Who Writes
   Together," *Kentucky Monthly*, www.kentuckymonthly.com/
   culture/people/the-couple-who-writes-together.
2. Quoted in Nancy Gibbs and Michael Duffy, "Ruth Graham,
   Soulmate to Billy, Dies," *Time*, June 14, 2007, http://content.time
   .com/time/nation/article/0,8599,1633197,00.html.

3. Ashleigh Slater, *Team Us: The Unifying Power of Grace, Commitment, and Cooperation in Marriage* (Chicago: Moody, 2014), 54.

4. Jasmine Holmes, Twitter post, 7:51 a.m., May 27, 2017, https://twitter.com/JasmineLHolmes/status/868479657456406528.

Chapter 8: The Setup for Success

1. Quoted in Don E. Fehrenbacher and Virginia Fehrenbacher, eds., *Recollected Words of Abraham Lincoln* (Stanford, CA: Stanford University Press, 1996), 50.

2. Billy Graham, *Unto the Hills*, 2nd ed. (1986; repr., Nashville: Nelson, 2010), 7.

3. Jennifer Smith, *Unveiled Wife: Embracing Intimacy with God and Your Husband* (Carol Stream, IL: Tyndale, 2015), 197.

4. Philip Yancey, *Prayer: Does It Make Any Difference?* (Grand Rapids: Zondervan, 2006), 210.

5. C. S. Lewis, *The Four Loves* (1960: repr., New York: Harcourt, Brace, 1991), 121.

6. Jackie Hill Perry, Twitter post, 4:02 p.m. July 3, 2017, https://twitter.com/JackieHillPerry/status/882011800182677506.

7. Stephen R. Covey, *Principle-Centered Leadership* (1990; repr., New York: Free Press, 2003), 49, italics original.

Chapter 9: Never Stop Starting Over

1. See "What's Wrong with the World?" American Chesterton Society, www.chesterton.org/wrong-with-world.

2. Cindy Beall, *Healing Your Marriage When Trust Is Broken: Finding Forgiveness and Restoration* (Eugene, OR: Harvest House, 2011), 37.

3. Anna Bahney, "Here's What Americans Are Spending on Weddings," *CNN Money,* January 16, 2018, http://money.cnn.com/2018/01/16/pf/wedding-cost/index.html.

4. See "Average Wedding Cost," Cost of Wedding, www.costofwedding.com.

Proverbs 31
MINISTRIES

ABOUT PROVERBS 31 MINISTRIES

If you were inspired by *Keep Showing Up* and desire to deepen your own personal relationship with Jesus Christ, I encourage you to connect with Proverbs 31 Ministries.

Proverbs 31 Ministries exists to be a trusted friend who will take you by the hand and walk by your side, leading you one step closer to the heart of God through:

- Free online daily devotions
- First 5 Bible study app
- Online Bible studies
- Podcast
- Daily radio program
- Books and resources

For more information about Proverbs 31 Ministries, visit www.Proverbs31.org.